WALKER & THE DARK

Mallikarjun B. Mulimani

Leadstart
INKSTATE

ISBN 978-93-5667-232-1

First published in India 2022 by Leadstart Inkstate
A brand of One Point Six Technologies Pvt. Ltd.

Unit no. 26, Ground Floor, A1, Shram Safalya,
Wadala Truck Terminal Road, Near Post Office,
Antop Hill, Mumbai – 400037.
Phone: +91 96999 33000
Email: info@leadstartcorp.com
www.leadstartcorp.com

Disclaimer: This is a work of fiction. All the names, characters, businesses, places, events and incidents in this book are either the product of the author's imagination or used in a fictitious manner. Any resemblance to actual persons, living or dead, or actual events is purely coincidental.

Editor: Sanjhee Gianchandani
Cover: Ilaya Raja
Layouts: Sathish Kumar

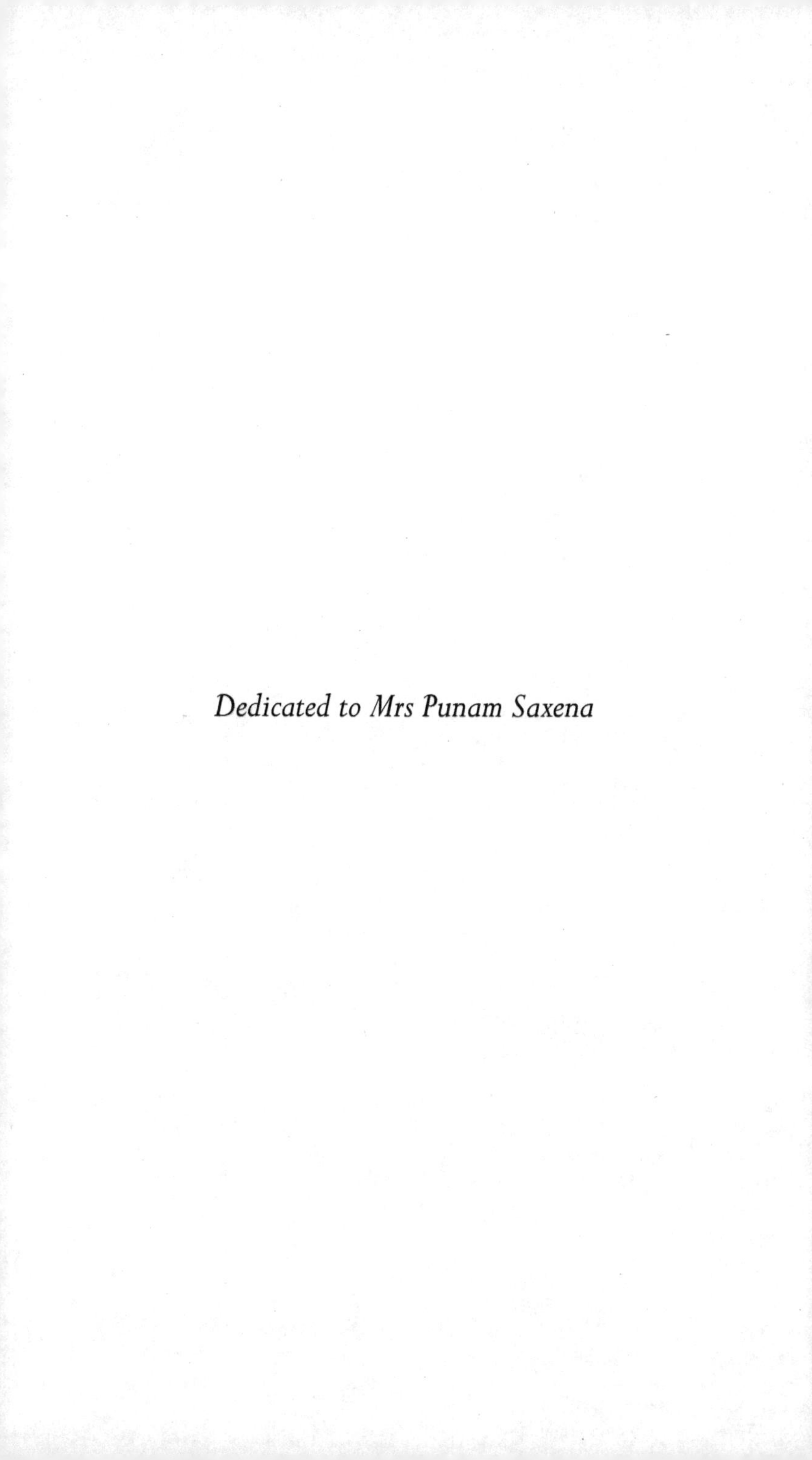

Dedicated to Mrs Punam Saxena

Contents

THE DARK

About the Author

Mallikarjun B. Mulimani is a versatile writer. He writes novellas, novels, and long and short poems including haikus. His books and style of writing, where brevity is the hallmark, influenced by his engineering background, are unique and highly acclaimed. His writings are crisp, carrying a theme and a message making them highly readable. So far, he has twenty-five books to his credit. They revolve around diverse themes: the psychology of humans and their milieu, God, love, sex, religion, the realization of self, life and death. They often touch the metaphysical domain.

Books by the Author

1. Do – The Fourth Musketeer of Lust, Love, and Life (Leadstart Publishing Pvt. Ltd., Mumbai, 2022)

2. Relevance of Swami Vivekananda in the Contemporary World (Sharada Book Depot, Bidar, 2022)

3. Death of a Philosopher (Olympia Publishers, London, 2022)

4. Whimsical Dice (Olympia Publishers, London, 2021)

5. Predator & Prey (Leadstart Publishing Pvt. Ltd., Mumbai, 2021)

6. Rivers (Writers Workshop, Kolkata, 2021)

7. Demystifying God, Eros and Bacchus (Olympia Publishers, London, 2020)

8. Life Unshackled – From Darkness to Light (Leadstart Publishing Pvt. Ltd., Mumbai, 2020)

9. Approaching Death (Writers Workshop, Kolkata, 2019)

10. A Mariachi & A Philosopher On Wheels – A Poem (Leadstart Publishing Pvt. Ltd., Mumbai, 2019)

11. A Writer's Zen (Leadstart Publishing Pvt. Ltd., Mumbai, 2018)

12. Selene – A Poem (Leadstart Publishing Pvt. Ltd., Mumbai, 2017)

13. Poems For Us (Leadstart Publishing Pvt. Ltd., Mumbai, 2017)

14. Poems To Myself (Leadstart Publishing Pvt. Ltd., Mumbai, 2017)

15. Alternative Haikus (Leadstart Publishing Pvt. Ltd., Mumbai, 2017)

16. Buddha In A Mercedes (Leadstart Publishing Pvt. Ltd., Mumbai, 2017)

17. Politics – A love Story (Leadstart Publishing Pvt. Ltd., Mumbai, 2016)

18. Bhakti Sans Religion – Dilemmas in the Search of One's True Inner Self (Leadstart Publishing Pvt. Ltd., Mumbai, 2016)

19. Star Ride to Nirvana (Leadstart Publishing Pvt. Ltd., Mumbai, 2015)

20. Dams across the Flow (Writers Workshop, Kolkata, 2015)

21. Victims Incorporated – Circles of Sub-consciousness (Current Publications, Agra, 2013)

22. What Happened to My Creativity (CreateSpace, USA, 2013)

23. Operation Epiphany – God's Journey on Earth (Writers Workshop, Kolkata, 2012)

24. The Holy Plumber and Other Stories (Writers Workshop, Kolkata, 2009)

25. Abstractions (Writers Workshop, Kolkata, 2007) (with digital art)

Acknowledgements

My parents' unwavering love, affection, encouragement, and most importantly, patience, have always enabled me to write. Thank you, mother and father.

WALKER

> **Men wanted to see a walker, hence, they saw Walker, the walker, not the man, the real Walker**

Hate

Should be a stateless

State

Congress

Of love's progress

The only success

When naked beauty streaks through you, be there for it in
your together moment, and nowhere else.

The moment is not a fragment.

Preface

Initially, did Walker have a teacher for his mission with its vision? No. Why? Because, a student inclined towards hell doesn't need a teacher. He was trying to capture what was already within him, freedom, and hence failed. Did Walker finally have a great teacher who set him free from himself? Yes. When two like minds meet, resonance will set them both free. But Walker can be forgiven, for if one leaves oneself, one is nobody, for one cannot be anybody else, then, what would be the purpose of such a one's life? So, one had better be oneself. Walker was, and eventually, his own path led him to his own freedom. Why did Walker and others suffer? Because, Walker's and everyone else's pain was that one's pain is one's to bear alone, and it is not at all masochistic to say that through our own suffering lies the only path that leads us to our own bliss. Walker, at the end of, whatever, had understood that listening to and chanting mantras of peace have no significant bearing upon one's inner peace if one doesn't block out the outside noise and go inwards towards one's peace silently calling out to one from within. To live amidst the noise without and be silent within, was the true peace that Walker finally realized. But was it always possible, for all, everywhere, with less than enough money to survive, needing more to barely survive, was a question the lucky Walker would never be able to answer for the unlucky walkers, whose feet bled as they walked on thorny unpaved roads unable to buy the cheapest of slippers, for Walker had left them to fend for themselves, having found his peace.

Walker's Quotes

About Reform

Walker was sitting in his third chair, the hardest with a straight back, yet soft enough to make him comfortable enough to think comfortably.

What freedom from others' thoughts does one need to think freely on one's own?

Can economic equality, the basic requisite for free thinking for all, be achieved when men are shrouded by the hate of one another's religious disparity?

Doesn't the God fallacy need to be eradicated if men are to achieve peace with one another?

It may be a communist low before a capitalist high, but the capitalist high will then be of creative communism, and nothing else.

If peaks keep on growing slenderly, chasms will be wide and vast.

About the Moment

Restrict your boundless energy to the present moment and exhilarate in it without frittering it away on past and future ones.

About Creation

If one says that the Creator who created this universe is self-created, then another can just as easily say that the universe is self-created, and progressing further, letting go of creation completely, come to the rational conclusion that there was no creation of anything at all, but that the universe always existed, in one form or another.

About Awareness

Awareness is the cumulative reaction of one's fertilization to one's cumulative senses' absorption of one's environment.

About Consciousness

Only the tangible is consciousness. Energy can be tangible through the medium it permeates.

About the Precious

Yearning for constancy in anything leads to utter destruction. For example, yearning for constancy in intoxication leads to addiction and then utter destruction. Anything in life, when kept rare, becomes precious.

About Courage

Speed bumps, pitfalls, and those pushing you towards disasters exist; however, if fear is eliminated from the mind, the only place where it exists, by being aware in the moment and following laws, the dangers are better dealt with when they come.

About Control

Bestriding a bridled horse is better than riding a mustang clutching onto its mane. Savages do that.

About the Little

Appreciate the little rats who help you sniff out your little inconsistencies. Spread the breadcrumbs for both of you in time and space to better reach out without overloading the both of you.

About Walker's Bathos

They hung me with a medal on a podium in an empty stadium.

About Walker's Magic

My life is one without magic or hope, and thus there is in it that hopeless magic.

About Solitude

A mind in seclusion grows exponentially, but to whose avail? It has to break free of its self-imposed bondage to be of the greater good, not caring about its exponential demise.

PART 1

WALKER

Vulture to Cow

Walker was a sphere. A sphere unto his own containing innumerable radii, from and to his centre. A confused holocaust in the making, and why had a simple yet complex answer. That the poor fellow was in love, in love with a love which would never ever respond to him, again, simply and complexly because, he, Walker, did not know what love was, for coming to Walker's defence, for the first time, nobody had given him the love he wanted, or more precisely, to be really fair to Walker, the love he deserved.

So, what happens to such a loveless person like Walker? There are two alternatives. One, that such a person commits suicide, or that person leads to mass suicide by way of inciting men to rush headlong into his mad ideas by leading them to believe that he is offering them freedom through annihilation, which all men want for one another, of who they believe to be their oppressors.

Unfortunately, for all, Walker did not commit suicide, but he galloped, towards himself, death, loveless.

What drives a few men born to gallop towards death, more others to maintain a gallop till death, and many more to meander in the hope that they will find a final happy solution to the finality of death and not ever meet a nothingness that they are so scared of?

Before jumping to answers, we must understand how men are typed into three groups to answer this three-parted question. The three groups are the fools, rebels, Walker and Walker's men, men of power, already being or quickly turning heinous Hyenas, sordid scavengers, Vultures, and cowards, Cows, respectively.

Where there are men of power, there will be rebels, fighting for the cowards, or as so many just assume, and assumption is a very dangerous thing.

The powerful men of power are in the middle of everything and rule the world without the necessity of anybody's help while the fools and the cowards on the opposite ends of the three-dimensional spectrum are hell-bent upon ruining each other as theirs is an asinine love, hate, love, relationship, while trying to annihilate and escape the powerful men of power.

It must be understood that for the first and third groups it is death which makes them behave the way they do throughout their lives after childhood when they start becoming more and more aware of death. While the third group starts getting scared of, confused about, and threatened by, death, the first starts getting excited about it, and excitement being a quality of the brave and adventurous, both qualities which spark off the quest for and a quick understanding of reality with a directing rational mind, the fools come to the rational conclusion that it is only nothingness that exists before birth and after death, and that consciousness is just an accident with a beginning and an end like everything else in the universe, including the universe too. The fools become fearless; no longer scared of death; this makes them insanely dangerous.

All this while, the cowards rush to religion, holy books, and philosophers, and start following them blindly without exercising their most important muscle, their brain. This makes the irrational cowards highly dangerous too, because they are worse off than animals without a mind of their own. At the same time, the cowards start hating the fools because the fools with their rationality and bravery, rational bravery, are a threat to their irrational comfortable idea of an afterlife, and the cowards who do not care a hoot for the qualities the concept of God stands for, but are interested only in furthering their puny and miserable lives are lost, for hate is never rational. It clouds minds to rational judgements very easily and quickly lends itself and the men holding it to servility. The rationality of the men supposedly fighting for irrational men is at the core of their love, hate, love relationship.

As for the men of power, one cannot look inside their armours of metal, armours which, instead of protecting their wearers against what can go in are meant to block what can go out, and though these clever men take in the ideas of those they want to rule, and rule because they craftily manipulate the ideas of those they want to rule, and rule, the true ideas of the rulers are never ever even slightly known to the ruled.

The fools are fools because being unafraid of death they gallop towards it, and are dangerous because again being unafraid of death, they try to force their ideologies on the rest using an iron fist. The cowards are cowards, and the reason they are dangerous is that they are a large mindless army led by godmen and foolish philosophers all scared of death and hence, galloping away from it, they rush headlong into the small band of brave fool fighters. The men of power, the rulers, stay away from these battles between the fools and cowards having realized that ruling's primary rule is to let those who they want to rule destroy each other so that they, the Vultures of war, can feed on dead men and their ideas and rule the wounded and exhausted rest.

However, from time to time, the fools gain a leader who thinks he is wiser than the rest of the fools, and this makes him the most dangerous fool of all fools, a dangerous fool who has the power to destroy, thinking he is helping his group's arch-enemies, the cowards, and also their rulers, the men of power, and this is the story of the greatest fool to date, Walker, who walked the fastest gallop over ideas and men within range of his directing rational mind and physically weak body.

The Vultures were the men of power gone soft owing to their undisputed ruling, wise mindless spineless ones, never exerting any effort to kill, just feeding on rotting flesh.

The Hyenas were the self-slaved soldiers of Vultures, laughing heinously, hysterically, in fear, frustration, excitement, in staccato bursts of machine gun fire, as they in large packs, especially at night, stole, ravaged, and killed, even Lions, using their incredibly powerful jaws having a bite force greater than that of Lions while finishing off any Lion cubs if present, too, but almost always feeding on Cows.

The Lions were the last few brave men left, who, and whose cubs, were being wiped-off by gangs of roaming Hyenas. The Lions were solitary creatures and hence easy prey for packs of Hyena predators.

The Cows were the cowards, men controlled and cultivated, and bred by Hyenas for food, for themselves as well as for their masters, the Vultures.

The Vultures didn't have to do a damned thing. The Hyenas enjoyed killing. The Lions were becoming extinct, and with the cowardly Cows unable to do a damned thing, the world was quickly decaying.

While there were men fighting, killing, and destroying, there were the wise old Owls and whimsical Butterflies creating, building, and establishing, science, philosophy, and art, constantly growing pillars upon which other men could keep on establishing and destroying their empires. These night-Owls and day-Butterflies were the only constant sanity within an ever-escalating insanity.

And then came Walker, Walker, with his inner circle, the circle of fools, led by the greatest fool, Walker himself, which comprised:

Commie: Walker's self-appointed commander-in-chief, his self-declared staunch supporter, who revolted at every step, revolting against Walker's 'creative' in both communism and eugenics, a hardliner.

Soldier: A mindless brute, who blindly followed and perfectly executed all orders of Walker's, without even a single question arising in his mind.

Thinker: The exact opposite of Soldier, Walker's alter ego, who did nothing but think and talk, a man of absolutely no action.

Adder: Soldier's understudy, she kept on adding to the number of men she had caused severe pain to by deceiving them, and then later, laid them open to be killed by Soldier.

Flower: An innocent, young, brave, idealistic, and pretty journalist, who, in her own small and frail craft, was walking upon a raging ocean with Walker, madly in love with him.

How had this coterie come to be?

Walker, after entering a narrow-minded home from behind, whose false doors of virtue, Adder, was lustfully advancing her wares, had bought them, and was quickly later, accosted by Soldier, demanding his share of her wares.

But Walker had not paid Soldier, instead, he had bought both him and his Adder, by promising them a share of his disaster, and, since, Walker's disaster was greater, greater than the disaster that Soldier and his Adder were currently after, they had both agreed to be a part of a greater disaster.

Thinker was a dissatisfied professor, who, when Walker had walked through his university campus, had started walking with him, along with Commie who had been a student leader in the same university, and since Commie had been more interested in rabble-rousing than studying, he had found in Walker, a greater leader through whom he could be a greater leader.

Flower was a delicate flower who had plucked herself out of her garden of journalism to record Walker in her journal with her pen of love.

Before the entire coterie had come to be, it had seemed to Soldier and his Adder (Adder, who was then also Walker's) that Walker once he had included the two inside his inner fortress was silently making them stand inside the iron gates to his impenetrable mind waiting for more conspirators, conspirators against whatever he was conspiring against, for both Soldier and Adder were but mindless weapons best used by letting them know nothing about what they would be entrapping and killing, and the two who knew at least this little much about themselves with conviction and happiness were proved right after Thinker and Commie were let in by them at the iron gates into Walker's mind. But even then, Walker had remained silent as far as the present priests in his inner sanctum sanctorum were concerned.

Soldier and Adder had found no cause to complain at the continued silence of Walker. Thinker had thought the same having been informed silently by the first two about Walker's silence with those whom he was letting in, into him. But Commie had been a different matter altogether. He had been a blasted nuisance to one and all concerned as a rabble-rouser where he had been before, and since here he was absolutely sure, which was absolutely true, that Walker had selected him for his vicious mouth which accentuated and amplified his vicious thoughts, he had started echoing them in Walker's impenetrable fortress now that he had been let in, but he was paid no attention to by anybody inside Walker's fortress, including Walker himself. Walker had walked abstruse and arcane routes until finally the iron gates of his mind had been crashed into, and destroyed by a pastel pink, suffused with a delicate white, fragile Flower. Walker, then immediately recovering, had barricaded his mind again, once and for all, with greater gates against all his enemies, with Flower, Thinker, Adder, Soldier, and Commie, all locked up within him in his mind-fortress and in that descending order.

Desert Walks and Talks

It was after noon when the six bullets in Satan's revolver, after walking since dawn to the beginning of a desert, were happily journeying over the uneasy desert blaspheming against its hellish heat. But the truck they were travelling in would have no truck with the disaster they were heading towards, and soon blew its own tyres. The six deserted the dead vehicle in the middle of a deserted desert and began to amble for they knew or rather thought unwisely that the whole world was their playground.

Walker had practised a strong silence with each and every one of the five fingers of his iron fist right from the moment the first had grown and progressed to the fifth full-grown, but now his tongue parched by the summer sun swung into action, "Speak! To me!"

It was Flower from whom the first wasp flew and stung Walker, "When are you going to stop walking and start galloping, Walker dear?" At this sudden painful sting, Walker yelled and spoke for only the second time in his iron-banded-together coterie, "Time destroys people who are impatient and squander unnecessarily their energies on what can't be changed at that moment, but dances a love dance with those who know how to wait, watch, and then dance at the right moment, with its transience," his yell being more precisely because of the "dear" at the end of Flower's question rather than the question itself.

Commie, who hated to be stung by not being the first to be stung or to sting, tried to sting, "Agreed, me and Flower with you, Walker, but why these others in our *Gymnasium of Champions*?" At which, Walker, brushing off Commie's broken sting with an easy careless mind replied, "One can learn at least something fine even from anything highly asinine. Very early in my writing career, I hated the word *stupid* for I found it to be really stupid giving itself justice and had come up with asinine write-ups trying to get irresponsible and frivolous readers to read and enjoy the responsible and serious Walker as I had realized that it took all kinds to write a book for to be read, one of which was, 'Multiple-sex gyms exist already because they fill all sexes with the necessary and extra adrenaline to work out more vigorously and build their bodies with more efficacy and efficiency, making such gyms more popular than single-sex gyms. But since this idea innovated from single-sex gyms, already exists, innovating further, if, like certain high-end pubs and discotheques, such already innovated gyms allow entry for only handsome males and all females of any kind, then they will become really popular and high-end gyms.' This was as asinine as I could ever get. Now here since you, Thinker, and I myself will find no entry into any of my innovated innovated gymnasiums, and Soldier, Flower, and Adder, will find no instruments, which are we, with which to work out and build themselves, completely, in those innovated innovated gymnasiums, we had all better stick together, forever. Every sinner can learn from any saint and every saint can learn from any sinner," without the prick having penetrated him.

The desert of death was conducive to Adder, and since now two had already had their turn with Walker, the impatient Adder hissed, "Why are you dressed like you are, Walker, in your white tee, black shorts, and grey slippers? Doesn't your attire send the wrong message that you really don't care truly about anything?"

Walker stomped his grey-clad foot on the hard sand, "Very often, the right action of a leader will send the wrong message to both his followers and detractors. Just wait and watch each and every one of my actions. Sooner or later, they will explain themselves to all."

He then extricated his estranged grey slipper from within the golden burning sands of time, and shaking it down lost more time by which time, as usual, Adder was followed by Soldier, "Don't worry about anything, Walker. With me always around you, your security is always guaranteed!"

Walker made Soldier beat a hasty retreat, "Two insecure people, you both, Soldier and Adder, getting together for security and then ruining your security together because of your combined insecurity, start preying upon other people's insecurity to rob their security. Glad to have you aboard with me, Soldier, but first understand your own weaknesses before trying to prey upon others', or the predator you might just as well become the prey. Let me tell you all about an incident from my younger years, which gave me great insight into the ways of the world. I had been eating pieces of a sweet fruit at my table when I had to leave for a full minute. When I came back, I found many very tiny ants scampering over my food. I, who was initially at a loss as to what to do, as I would not be able to wash off the innumerable ants from my tiny pieces of fruit without ruining them, finally decided to just go ahead with my eating, fruit and ants both. To my great surprise, I found immediately after relishing my second piece of ant-covered fruit that there was not even a single ant left on the plate containing my remaining pieces of fruit. I had an "epiphany": I had been the predator eating my fruit. Then the ants had turned predator on me and my fruit, but after I, the prey, turned predator, the ants became an easy prey proving that disgusting deeds have to be done to enjoy one's food. Ha-ha!"

By the time Walker had finished poisoning the pristine desert with his vicious words of predator and prey, a desert death adder had added a lizard to its being.

Soldier stopped walking, clicked his heels, and gave Walker a smart salute, while Adder, walking beside Walker, leaned over and kissed him on his cheek.

Flower was not at all impressed, and Thinker, like thinking comes last to most, finally took his turn, "What do you think, Walker?"

Walker thought aloud, "Just before dawn today, a messenger informed me of the death of my Godfather.

"Death, like life, teaches us many things. Among them, is equality, I truly believe.

"Most may think I have an obsession with death, but hopefully one day all will understand my problems, but not anytime soon I promise you.

"For Walker, walking it was again at dawn.

"I would like to believe that what in a discarded Foreword by me for one of my old books, *Approaching Death*, written by the great old man containing as one of its most profound statements, 'Walker has written *Approaching Death*, but I believe that it is time for him to start writing about, *approaching life…*' is what Walker is walking.

"It is not a person's death, but how it affects one saddens one. But today, I am laughing like no one probably has before, for myself and my intrusion along with the great-no-more-man, into what it was that made life, life, possessed by the laugh he had rivalled only by that of mine, during yesterdays makes me proud today. The power he gave me to laugh with my whole heart not caring about who saw our jugulars in our throats opened wide to swallow life, and then give it out enriched with our wholehearted enthusiasm, not caring about who was spinning reality to slit our jugulars, was the life we lived. After I heard of his death, I understood more clearly that since the way you live is the way you die, as he died laughing at life, he died laughing at death too, and hopefully I, too, will die in such a manner supreme."

Despite the wretched desert, Flower bloomed further, "You love the wretched. Don't you, Walker? After all, you are incessantly walking for them!"

But Walker wilted, "I have forgotten what it is to truly kiss, and here I am, the wretched, trying to solve the wretched problem of the wretched!"

Flower and Adder looked at each other spitting venom and nectar.

Thinker wondered with his tongue, "Somebody gave me Walker's old visiting card once. I wondered then and am still wondering now what the only two embossed, golden upon black background words meant…"

Thinker and Walker were blazing away in the burning desert.

Walker reminisced for the benefit of all, "The *ZAP WORKS* on my Veni, Vidi, Vici card stood for *Zeal, Analysis, Perseverance WORKS*. Something I had come up with during my younger days instantaneously when it had been required as if I had been zapped with creativity. That instantaneous creativity is what I have always lived by since then and hence, my old card."

Commie caught fire.

"Enough of just thinking, talking, and walking! Let us start acting!" shouted Commie and he was backed up by Soldier's, "Yes! Let's kill us some people!"

Soldier was beginning to faintly see with whom a productive future for him lay.

Walker was not blind to anything except his own mistakes, and he said calmly but firmly, "The idea has to be attacked, not the people who hold the idea for if one kills one person or more who hold the idea, the idea will still remain alive within innumerable others who hold the same idea. But if one kills the idea itself, all the people holding the same idea will have been killed. But this idea is meant to be taken in a very positive sense in all ways, for example, attack poverty, not the poor… This is creative communism at its best."

Commie bridled upon hearing the word, 'creative', adjectivizing his beloved communism.

But Adder was softer, "What is creativity, Walker?"

"'Go, Ego!' and 'Go, Ego, Go!' and 'Nothing like work!' and 'Nothing like work, if the work is creative!'" are examples of creativity, my dear, replied Walker softly.

Flower was softer than Adder, "How to leave the *I*, and still survive?"

Walker gushed, "Simply *Be*."

The innumerable hot sands of time were being crushed away under the cold harsh footsteps of the six.

Thinker and Walker entered into deviating dialogues with Thinker beginning, "Life doesn't wait. Does it?"

"Not for anyone."

"What is refining?"

"One can only refine oneself, and no other…"

"Who is the best reader for one's work?"

"One oneself is, and nothing like it. However, many a time one oneself is unable to be… Everyone needs a friend, other than one oneself… Life is always beautiful with another beautiful mind!"

"Isn't self-love enough?"

"Yes, it is! But it can be reached only in the latter part of one's life once all cobwebs in the mind have been melted away by its growing flames of strength, but until that supreme moment, it's never wrong to be helped on the way towards self-love by a whimsical other! No man or woman can be completely alone almost till the end."

"How tough was writing for you, Walker?"

"What I proposed was tough love for both myself and my writing, but I often allowed myself to ride my unicorn over my own rainbows!"

"How did other men strengthen you, Walker?"

"Men, who are loved by men with directing rational minds, can do proactive damage to the latter by convincing them that even the most rational minds tend to find the irrational rational in the coincidental. Thankfully, I was not scarred as I drew my strength from their weakness."

Walker continued and asked, "What made you leave your old organization and become part of mine, Thinker?"

Thinker emerged from his bunker, "An organization is its people, and people are their organization, each responsible for the other. If even a single person makes a mistake, his organization can be blamed, and if the organization makes a mistake, all its people can be blamed. I was not willing to take the blame for my old organization's and my co-workers' rampant corruption and stupidity, and in you, Walker, I found a thinker with a directing rational mind. Thank you for having me."

Flower sighted water, an oasis amidst men's parched thinking walled in by dry sand dunes of ideas, which can be reshaped by any strong wind at any time.

Ideas will keep on changing, thinking will remain thirsting, and the only stuff of life lies deep within our deserts.

After the coterie drank and made camp, Flower, the journalist, sent out a fragrance, "What are your views on freedom and love, Walker?"

Walker stared straight ahead as he answered, "Most people are beasts latched in behind bars and lacking the spirit to think and be free. If one, a beast too, but a different breed of beast, pacing up and down thinking in one's own cage on figuring out how to escape, finally escapes by unlatching the simple latch of one's own cage that was holding one in without either a lock or a key, which is the same for all the others' cages, and then, progresses to unlatch the cages of innumerable mindless others, the hungry brutes who have spent their time sleeping in their own cages, once they are set free, will find nothing better to do than feed upon the flesh of their liberator, who too, is hungry, but for more knowledge of freedom.

"Love needs to be shown, not only intangibly given.

"Only a thing, really lost, has any true meaning.

"It was a warm summer afternoon. After a cool and fragrant zephyr had blown upon my face, I had suddenly realized, that I was in love with life, and therefore, her too, once more disregarding all the lifelessness of life; however, my greatest realization upon the topic of love is that *Love has nothing to do with happiness.* Therefore, I am happy with no love, even straying my way."

While Flower was wondering, *What in hell is wrong with this bloke?* Commie taunted Walker, "Hate, according to you, O beloved leader?"

Walker calmly replied, "A man gets angry simply because of his own deficiencies, and none others'.

"There is a thin green-red line between being at peace and being ineffective, for while it is most important that one doesn't lose one's calm, never ever giving into anger, hate, and rage, it is more important that one uses one's energy, an energy that would be wasted by indulging in anger, hate, and rage, to coldly and calculatedly douse completely others' anger, hate, and rage. While this is easier said than done, nothing is improbable if one takes one's each and every moment at a time and lets his superconsciousness do the trick for him with no past or future, other than those integrated unconsciously within his superconsciousness of the moment playing any part in his moment, leaving him completely free to be absolutely peacefully free.

"Commie, don't satisfy your hate, for it is very easily satisfied initially, but finally your hate will end up annihilating primarily yourself, and then all your loved ones as well."

The blood-red sun, tired of its heat heating the desert, was about to turn in for the night, but already a fire had been set blazing to replace it by the men who could not sleep and wouldn't be satisfied with the moon.

In this romantic setting, Adder coyly added her question, "Your Johnny, me, and music, Walker?"

Walker laughed, "Unless one is really enlightened, one cannot be truly enlightened.

"Prostitutes are noble women who get paid to pay for the sins of nobler women.

"Music releases the killer-beast from within its screwed-up cage to dance a tango with life, for all in one way or another are dancing a tango, in one form or another, with either a somebody or something other."

The tone had been set for talking throughout the night.

Thinker was clever, "Reality and life, Walker?

Walker was grave as he said, "Life is an accident of life. Our great body, within it the physical mind, is an accident too. Ordinary people think, *If this had happened or not happened, we would be happy or unhappy*. But, if one starts to really observe life, one would realize that one would be either happy or unhappy in any reality, which would be different from innumerable other realities, irrespective of what happened or didn't. Absurd life would have progressed just the same irrespective of whether one was happy or unhappy. It is our absurd thinking and unnecessary imagination that ascribes only one path to life.

"The ordinary are only worried about surviving, not living, but then again, who will the intellectuals live with if they out-intellectualize all non-intellectuals into dying, for even two intellectuals in the same room are one too many to bear by anyone in the room, including the two intellectual gangsters themselves!"

The peaks of the warming fire roared into the brilliant stars enveloped by the chilly night.

Soldier asked Walker sadly, looking at Adder, "Do you recognize me, Walker? If you don't, I don't exist, then how can I ever be with someone completely?"

Walker was not soft, "No one need recognize one if one recognizes oneself.

"Absorbing and leaking into are the only two methods of being one with everyone, Soldier, be strong man!"

Soldier said pitifully, "You set too fast a pace, Walker…"

Walker quickened his pace, "If one doesn't lose to oneself, no one else can make that one lose to them.

"And, Soldier, life should be a sprint, not a marathon. You, of all people, must be aware of that. Soft others set a soft pace for themselves, and therefore, most, will finish the *Marathon of Life*, most, losing. But I, Walker, have set the fastest pace I can for myself, and as I have galloped unbridled till now, and will certainly do the same in the future, I will certainly win the sprint against myself, for there are no comparable others in Walker's life. I know you all will unhesitatingly do the same."

Commie threw the body of a slain and drunk coconut into the flames.

Thinker chuckled, "They said you were the most repressed and hence the most dangerous, Walker. I never believed them!"

Walker added his chuckle to Adder's, "Repressed people are certainly the most dangerous, and therefore, I can be called the least dangerous of all men, for if I am not anything, it is repressed, even in the least, and this is a good, statement-point, in my favour.

"As for *they* and *them*, they have never understood this: *Never get ahead of others, or for that matter even yourself, for you will never ever know what others are thinking, or what they will think next, and even where you yourself are concerned, what you will think next will also be forever beyond you, as each and every moment is but transient.*

"And I *am* dangerous in my own way simply because of this: *Walker is a warrior who dismantles his would-be attackers even before they have begun to form and shape their attacks in their minds, simply because he believes that no preparation is the best preparation, thus leaving him free of prejudices when the time comes for the actual battles with freedom, being the fountainhead of victory."*

The flames roared.

Flower, tired of the complex Walker, could contain herself no more and as a white petal of a teardrop fell from her pink bloom cried, "What is your problem, Walker?"

Walker was aghast, but tried to keep up appearances, "I am but an observer, who derives absolutely no pleasure from my observing the ghastly stuff of life in order to understand and then eradicate it, for I am no sadist.

"If you must know, Flower, I wish in my heart of hearts sometimes, that is, when I find the heart to do so, that there is an afterlife in which justice will be done to me and my love, but always immediately after these moments, I consider my weakest, I again realize that justice is mine to give, and not to receive, in the only life I and all else have."

The flames had roared more and more as Commie had kept on slaying coconuts, drinking, and throwing their bodies into their funeral pyre.

"More, Walker, more!" chanted Adder.

Walker was on a roll, "Why, all my ridiculous nonsense, can probably be gleaned from one of my write-ups which went something like this, 'When the person, to whom you have given all the love you had, asks you to take back all the photographs of you together, taken in the best of times, and also all the enchanting gifts you had given in the best of times, during your, as proved only later, only your best of times, the terrible question arises, "Is my love asking me to take back the love I had given, and how can I do it, let alone think of it?" and the answer is simple, "I have to become Walker! I have to walk away from the hell that is earth into a heaven of my own making…"', and, finally finding my answer, I, Walker, had walked."

Commie had slain, drunk, and burnt his last coconut. He shouted, "Enough of love! Talk about true freedom, Walker!"

Walker was only too happy to move away from disastrous talk, "All right. True freedom comes when everything one does, which may be okay or not okay in others' opinions, is simply okay by one, for one's freedom is not others' to give, but one's to realize."

"Explain!" was the next shout.

"All right. For example, when one meets a person of a culture different from one's, and one does not feel oneself obligated to greet that person in the manner of the other's culture, nor does one feel the obligation to stick to the culture one has been brought up in, but greets that person in a manner which instantaneously shoots up into one's mind in that transient moment, then one really is living one's life in the moment, free, free even from oneself. No preparation is the best preparation."

Commie, who had still not understood, sulked audibly, "Why do you taunt death, O immortal deliverer?"

Walker roared angrily with the flames missing bodies to devour, "Walker taunts death to feel free of it; fear never stands a chance against Walker's death wish."

The flames had fallen deathly silent, a silence which was broken by Thinker's sing-song voice causing them to dance again, "Be strong, not arrogant, and never ever rude.

"Be detached, not aloof, and never ever needy.

"Be always calm and kind, but never ever servile, and if the time comes, which it certainly will sooner than later, vamoose."

The bee of immortality had settled upon Flower, who asked, "Thinker, can you please explain the immortal mind?"

Thinker was only too happy to share his thoughts, "The mind, what exactly is the mind? The mind, which is the physical brain, that one fine day dies, and causes to die with it the thoughts and ideas that it had gleaned, ingested, and assimilated fully, and these being the intangible manure to the tangible soil of the physical brain had caused new evolved towering trees to grow with the seeds of one's creativity? Yes, in harsh reality, yes, if there had been no unconditioned explorers of seas of thoughts and ideas searching for undiscovered continents with newly evolved forests of thoughts and ideas, to discover one and one's worth, while one was still alive or dead, and with their vison made it their mission to help one gift one's self-created gifts to the rest of the world, and the harsh truthful reality is that there are not many such unconditioned explorers, and therefore of what use was the existence of one's mind without the prize of immortality for its having run the race of life, having won or lost? Everything exists, even the dead brain, in one way or another, in the universe, but the immortality of one's mind is assured through the sacrifice of all that one cherishes, even the freedom of one's peace, by allowing other men, who would want to desperately cut down one's forest to build their homes and fill their fireplaces with the myriad branches of one's thoughts and ideas growing in myriad directions in myriad ways, and finally chopping down the trunks of one's multidimensional being want to make barstools and feel secure and supreme in their tiny cramped inns and homes of tiny cramped thoughts and ideas, to satisfy their asinine desires, during one's painful life itself, with one not even hoping that someday these mediocre men will realize what they have done, what they are missing, and finally what they have wanted desperately to kill... So, what is it that will be killed, and what exactly are the seeds of one's creativity? Simply put, who is one? Is one the progeny of one's parents, the student of one's teachers, the love of one's love, the father of one's children? Who is one? One's answer is that, one is all, and not one, one is the universe, and one is immortal, as long as the universe is immortal. Thank you, Walker."

For the very first time, in the dead of the night, all were well and truly convinced about why Thinker was called Thinker. But none, except Walker, clearly understood why Thinker had thanked Walker at the end of his enlightening speech.

By now, Adder was bored out of her seductive mind, and she purred, "Talk about your Johnny, Walker…"

Walker sighed, "I cannot relax; even, and especially, after a drink, My mind is always running the thinking race against itself to win," and quickly bringing his Johnny out from his backpack, took a quick gulp, and shaking his head to make sure the firewater entered even the darkest and deepest dungeons of his brain, continued, fiercely, "It is known that, 'The brightest flame burns quickest', and innovating, if the spirit of the flame is fed by spirit, not only will the lonely candle in the candelabra stand no chance of surviving, but the entire candelabra itself will melt in the flame turned inferno's ferocity."

Adder squealed with delight, and hugging Walker's arm, snatched Johnny from his hand, and taking a gulp, trilled, "Females from Venus, are they looking at the Shining Sun or a relatively tepid Mars, compared to both Venus and Mercury? You are definitely not of Earth, dearest Walker!"

Commie, who wanted to be the Sun, got very angry, "Mercurial atmosphere, eh! Do we need all and all this, Walker!"

Thinker laughed, "We all need all to be all, the universe."

Flower flamed a brilliant red, "Who all and what all are you afraid of, Commie?"

Commie snorted, "I am not afraid of anybody or anything!"

Thinker, who had been laughing silently all the while, asked rhetorically, "Does one truly know what being afraid actually is?" and continued, "'Why and when is a man afraid?' has the answer, 'Because and when he doesn't adhere to the Truth.' This begs the question, 'What is the Truth?' which has the simple answer, which is not the answer, but the Truth that, 'Each man has his own truth,' which again begs the question, 'So, why is he afraid?' and the answer is, 'Because he does not know his own truth,' so going again, 'What is a man's own truth,' and the simple answer again is, 'If the man is self-aware, which is nothing difficult, then his truth can be anything or everything, and all he has to do to realize his own truth is to simply accept himself for himself, as he is without external influence,' and then, finally, if a man accepts this truth, which is the only Truth, he will be free of fear, fear of himself, which is the only and worst fear, and he will be free. But now comes desire, but desire is something, which if controlled and used wisely, will set a man freer if there is anything like more freedom that is."

"Are you afraid now, Commie?" smiled Flower, who had gone back to her white and pink.

Commie, who had gone pale in front of blazing flames, hesitated and answered, shakily, "No…"

Walker said gently to Commie, "Dear Commie, you are with us for a reason. Let us know your exalted ideas too."

Commie suddenly brightened up, brighter than the fire around which the six were sitting and started sailing smoothly, "It is only the moneyed who can even dare to think of true freedom, for even to get to the point of thinking about freedom requires the base of solid money from which one can launch oneself towards freedom.

"One is walking on roads built by tremendous others who had an iron will to cut down mountains and make paths for others towards freedom, and I ask weak infantile men, 'Pray, which stone have you moved on the path to freedom for humanity?'

"War of anything, mainly ideas, is dispersion and then incursion."

Everybody applauded Commie, except Thinker, who again laughed, "True enlightenment is ascending towards discarding, and then descending towards accepting, all. A descending which is the true ascending when almost all people are stuck in false ascending and will get nowhere. Are you truly enlightened, Commie?"

Commie flamed, "What have you got against me, Thinker? You never liked me, even in our once university!"

Thinker was calm, "If one doesn't accept Life for what it truly is, one is bound to be rejected by Life like in all other lesser relationships."

Flower added, looking wistfully at Walker on whose face shades of flames were dancing, "Don't lose yourself trying to be somebody else to please somebody else when there will always be somebody else who will accept you for yourself."

Walker pretended not to notice, either Flower's look, or her words, for Walker was a stickler who loved to stick to the older, on some matters at least.

But Flower went on, doggedly, "Pathways at a tangent to the whole, pathways to dreams, are made of this... Eden, right here right now."

Walker kept on looking straight ahead at his Eden in flames, with his ears expressionless.

Flower gave a small cry, "If one doesn't want a gift, one should gift it back, but retain its essence, to be truly gifted," and started sobbing softly.

Walker said, snatching an old memory out of the blue, "When a competitor, someone who upon beholding my imitation Parker brought his similar one out, I used to happily say, 'I had an original gold one once, but which my golden friends stole, so I am happy to be left with an imitation, for imitation is the golden rule of life.'"

Adder came to sit beside her rival, "What life are you talking about, dear emotionless Walker?"

Walker was not to be deterred from walking with his pen and paper, "Walker's books were almost always very short, for everything should be short, like short life itself where one needs to explore all and digest all, within a short time.

"What we were before birth we will be after death. There is no fear in this, and this is my life.

"About emotion: *Emotion, is the intangible volatile fuel in our tangible staid beings of domestic cars, which, if sparked off by the right spark, can turn them into race-cars striving to win without caring a damn about whether they win or not, for they would already have won the moment they started upon the race with a resolute intention to win.*"

Thinker laughed again, "Understanding all makes one all the more dangerous to all," and this time was joined in his laughing by Commie.

Soldier, who had become slightly wise after listening to all the wise and asinine dialogues of wise others, had painstakingly formulated a wise statement of his own, "To be completely free, one needs to be absolutely okey-dokey with doing anything and everything, while maintaining one's peace both before and after the doing of one's desired deed, which can be anything and everything."

Thinker could not stop laughing at his own wit, "Mental satisfaction is more pleasurable than the physical, simply because of the jealousy that it instigates in the physical, and one always wants to be one up on all."

Walker did not laugh, "When one is depressed, especially when one was younger and everything around one made one feel that one was missing that precious something, simply because one had not done anything to become something, to satisfy one's craving for world domination, either physical or mental domination over all men, which is the innate craving of all men, one feels really depressed, and this depression can only be alleviated by the drugs of 'Letting Go'.

"When one has to hold something, for example, anything, with one's painful diseased hand, and then, when one starts to realize that even pain can be transformed into everything enjoyable, beauty, then one is letting go of even pain and is experiencing the bliss of, 'Letting Go', pain being the path towards realizing one's happiness, and simply progressing further, why hold onto anything at all, even oneself?"

Thinker stopped laughing, and said seriously, but again rhetorically, "Yes, in one's quest for happiness, if one doesn't truly know Yin, how will one be able to recognize, understand, and accept, Yang when it comes to becoming truly happy?"

The flames were fed by Commie so that they could survive the enlightened dialogues of those around them as others quenched their thirsts with more coconuts. The night was neither happy, nor sad, but only cold. The laughing stars did not give a damn about what was happening under them. There had been no moon.

Walker had been a writer who had written for himself simply because in all probability no one else had understood what he was writing, and what for whom, but he had been happy with what had been dished out to him by himself, and since he had to eat to survive, he had been happy cooking for himself and eating what he deserved; however, unknown to him, a much younger Flower had been stalking his work, as a result of which when she had come to know that Walker had given up writing and started walking, at the first available opportunity, she had plucked herself out of her garden of journalism to try and bloom anew in a garden which she hoped to grow and tend for him.

Flower said quietly, "You are brutally honest, Walker, but to be so is to be sadly lonely and happy with only honesty for company."

Walker smiled, "We see only what we want to see, but to truly be, we have to truly see not only others as they themselves see, but also ourselves as we truly are disregarding the saying, 'Do not take anything at face value', for it is best to put our trust in that which others want us to see, for in all probability that is what they truly want to be, and therefore, try to show their true self to us so that we can all fall in love with one another."

Thinker smiled back, "The grunting heaving beast is dying, eking out its last thoughts, transforming them into beautiful words, but does the world have even the slightest inkling as to the true meaning of beauty?"

Adder spat, "How do you manage to come up with these stupid questions of wisdom, Thinker?"

Thinker laughed, "Anything and everything unsublime can trigger sublime thoughts, which only have to be put into sensible words to make it easy for the insensible to comprehend.

"Most people, with their asinine emotions, trigger profound revelations, for a few others who are on the path leading towards wisdom."

Adder was about to bite when Walker brought out his antivenom, "Understanding the cutting boundaries between domains is essential for ascendance in one's own domain, and then for conquering other domains."

"What!?" was the simultaneous cry by Adder and Thinker which went unanswered by Walker.

It will be dawn soon, announced the desert night which had been unsuccessful in getting its guests into its sandy beds.

Flower suddenly flowered, "Can man ever be an infinite eternal God, and thus, finally happy?"

Walker decided to pluck a flower, "No man, no matter how much he understands, will ever be happy in his only transient life as it simply doesn't span infinity and eternity which he is trying to comprehend and encapsulate within his short life, unless he lives in the moment where there is absolutely no necessity of such a hopeless undertaking of such a hopeless understanding, as he is both the infinite and the eternal in his dimensionless transient moment, God, and finally, happy."

Adder snuggled up to Walker who did not object, "You are God, Walker, in heaven."

Walker, wistfully looked at Flower, whose gaze was fixed on the infinity in the flames, "I created myself out of the hellish creations of others for themselves and others, and now, I am in my heaven, but is there anyone else with me here, *here* in *my* heaven, anyone? Maybe, this is in Truth my hell which I have created for myself using my abundant and reckless creativity."

Adder cooed, "I am, Walker, I am! In heaven, hell, or earth, or all three, your choice," while Flower closed her eyes encapsulating both infinity and eternity in her dimensionless transient moment and spoke more softly than Adder, "True living is to truly cut off from all others', and living within the seeking of one's being."

"Why aren't we being more proactive?" Commie grunted.

"If one becomes proud of rejecting everything, he had better become aware that he is accepting nothing," snorted Thinker.

Commie cried, "Have your way, Thinker! Hurt me as and when you will. I can't fight you!"

Thinker suddenly became sympathetic towards the younger one, "Let me help you, Commie.

"If one, a being, becomes a non-being, then the blind arrows that others shoot at one will have no target to find and pierce, to harm one, and one will have become truly invincible.

"If I remove my armour and expose myself completely, none will have any arrows in their quivers or swords in their scabbards to kill the naked me."

Commie calmed down, "You truly are the Thinker, Thinker. Thank you for your creative advice. But let me also state that creativity keeps on dying when one keeps on repeating anything."

Thinker fell sadly silent.

Flower took pity on Thinker, "Be creative once more, and tell us all creatively why you left your position at the university, Thinker."

Thinker beamed, "If one, both one's own master and one's own servant, the captain of one's ship and also the last deckhand, has no work to do, meaning not having any work to give to too, then the ship comes to a standstill in the middle of the ocean of life, which is death.

"Everyone and everything about my once university reeked of death," and again fell sadly silent.

Commie flared up, "I was there, wasn't I? And I am here now, aren't I? Am I a walking corpse? You were blind then, and you are blind now. You were living your myth then, as you are living your own myth now!"

Walker was complexly contradictory, "I too am indeed creating my own myths, but then again, who isn't? And as myths are nothing but myths, like everything we construct to bear and survive reality, which none of us know is what, the only path for us to take is to strongly believe in our own myths till the day we die, so that our life would have been lived in strength with a strong purpose, with life itself being a myth created by the amalgamation of all the myths of all those living life."

Walker never understood why he was not understood, most of the times, by the ordinary.

Thinker came back to his boisterous self, "I am not at all creative, Commie, and you know why? It is because the less one knows, the more creative one is, for then, one has innumerable domains unsullied by others' interpretations of reality to explore, understand, and innovate, create."

Commie laughed, "Both you and Walker, Thinker, like your overkills in all aspects of life, don't you both!"

Walker joined in the laughter, "Creativity is a quirk!" He then pulled out a white cigar from a black case, and bending forward into the scorching flames, lighted it and started puffing away all the nonsensical dialogues that had taken place.

No more was Walker wearing pink Maya goggles, and hence, had transformed their staid old home into a supremely better and aesthetic one, one of practical use, where he kept his cigars painted white by him on and surrounded by black velvet, but since white doesn't stop black from being black, he had gone ahead and painted the outside of the pink case black to remind himself, each time he wanted a cigar, as to what he was getting into. But Walker's motto, since his teenage years, had always been, 'No Limits No Regrets' – one clutches at straws, doesn't one? – and hence, he went on slowly murdering himself.

Adder bummed a cigar off Walker, and trying to blow white clouds into dark clouds, asked the night-sky, "Why wine for artists, Walker?"

Walker joined her in gazing up, "Dear, why wine for artists has the answer that it is fermented fruit, grapes turning into wine, that keeps the creativity of the fruity going on and on and on…"

Laughter echoed amidst the six giants.

Soldier wistfully said, "One has to be really crazy to live in and survive this crazy world, and the good ones wouldn't have it any other way. I wish I was crazy!"

Adder's gun shot with a puff of smoke, "What makes you think you are good and not crazy!"

Walker tried to douse the burning wound in Soldier, "One should be extremely careful of what one desperately wishes for, for more often than not such wishes come true, and notwithstanding the fact that a wish is something one truly wants, or why else would one wish, it is but the unfortunate truth that one most of the times doesn't truly know what one wants, and therefore, one is more often than not critically injured by one's wishing without truly thinking, and stands as an ugly symbol of one's dark wishing."

Soldier let out a deep sigh, "Then, then when then comes, let me wish properly. Imagination is a curse for you people."

Thinker chuckled, "At any point in time, imagination is very important. However, it is more important, as one progresses in time and space, to acknowledge immediately, facts presenting themselves in the present, facts falsifying one's imaginations in the past, to accept one's mistakes, and correcting the foundations of one's imaginations, which to most is an impossibility, progress with an evolved imagination that has obviously changed direction, knowing and being happy with the fact that one doesn't truly know one's temporary destinations until the permanent one of death."

Commie attacked, "Walker, you are giving Thinker too much freedom. He is attacking Soldier now!"

Walker smiled, "Freedom, without understanding freedom, leads to destruction."

Thinker, was in his own free freewheeling world, "Anything and everything should make one think deeply about anything and everything, helping one towards a complete understanding.

"A still ocean, without disturbing forces, conflicts, conflicts between the Yin and Yang, conflicts which push us to rise above our conflicts, without currents and winds of change, without the sun and the moon, all which cause the crests and troughs of waves, is but dead, not allowing one's ship to progress towards any destination."

The fire was dying, but it did not matter, for the dawn was very close to dawning.

Flower asked, "Walker, when is one really free?"

Walker replied quietly, "When one feels no need to do anything, upon the occurrence of any something, one is really free of everything."

Commie sneered, "Apathy is the greatest disease of the body and mind, the plague itself."

Thinker came back, "Ah! Opposite views… Any change is beautiful, if taken completely in, without rationalizing for or against it."

Commie was indefatigable in his fruitless attacks, "You are the ultimate Guru, aren't you, Thinker!"

Commie's arrow did not hit Thinker, who said, "Nobody can be anybody's Guru after a certain stage, a stage after which one is not only fully capable of being one's own guru, but should be and has to be. But unfortunately, it is almost always never the case with students remaining students and never ever transcending."

Flower was tired of the two unequal warriors. She posed a long-withheld question to Walker, "Why walking after writing, Walker?"

Walker sighed, "A midlife crisis around forty is not to be avoided, but desired as it surely will shred one's past, and making the shreds the manure in one's freshened mind-field, enable one to grow evolved towering trees of the future."

Flower laughed gaily, "Yes, if nothing is happening in one's life, then that nothing is the most dangerous something."

"Enough! Listen to me, you mindless philosophers!" shouted Commie, and went ahead, "If those who don't have don't follow the rules as a result of them wanting to have more, then the haves will also break the rules to have more. Thus, it is imperative that none must be allowed to have what they desire, only initially, so that finally all can have what they need as a result of rules being enforced with severity upon everybody."

Walker, who was listening intently, softly said, "Go ahead, Commie."

Commie went ahead, "Luxury is showering in abundant water, where innumerable drops directly hit the smooth tiles of the bathroom floor, and flow away into the drain without having washed off even a single grain of dirt, tainting the rich, while poverty is using every drop of tears to try and wash away the dirt of poverty, tainting one, without one not having done anything to stain oneself with the taint of poverty."

"Go on."

"Most people's minds are like the insides of public toilets, where in the comfort of their privacy, they feel they can scribble their crap and defile the privacy of the public."

"Thank you, Commie, enough for now."

The flames had completely died out, and it was still not light.

"Get real homie!" said Thinker to Commie.

Commie, whose nerves were frayed, cut through their last strands, "People believe what they want to believe, make it real!

"You, Thinker, a hereditary professor, think that you can lowball me, a less-than-ordinary man, born from low balls! Answer me, how much is one's fertilization, and by whom the fertilization, actually important to the mind of one in one's environment? And, since you people say that a man is both, and nothing except, his fertilization and environment, to all logical purposes, you Thinker, are my half-father, for you were the major player in my constructive environment, so, sir, why in hell are you hell-bent upon browbeating your half-son?"

The cold silence of a hell whose roaring infernos had frozen fell upon the party of slithering six.

Soldier quickly moved towards Adder and tightly hugged her to keep her warm amidst the chilling silence of words, immediately following which, she broke into hot sobs, "One can buy a body, but not a mind. And even if a mind can be bought, it will be of no use, for it will no longer be free," at which, Soldier, who had instantaneously become wise by years, spoke comfortingly, "If you relish the present moment, your whole past is vindicated, and if the present moment is destroyed by you, your whole past and future are both futile."

The indefatigable Thinker began again, expounding his thoughts, thoughts which seemed to have thoughts about each and every thought, "Even though the past *was* real, it *is* now just a memory. The actions, pains, and pleasures in it exist only in the mind, and if the memory is completely destroyed, by any means, the past completely ceases to exist. And even though the physical manifestations of past actions continue to exist, for example, the scars on one's body, if one looks at the scars, with absolutely no memory of when, how, and why they came into being, there is absolutely no pain in the present. Therefore, it becomes our duty towards ourselves to completely destroy the past memories which cause us pain in the present and will continue to do so in the future if they are not completely rooted out and got rid of, by any means necessary, so that both our present and future will be blissful."

Everyone was getting on one another's nerves by now, not even excepting Walker, who actually, since he was the so-called leader, the most screwed-up by his and his followers' thoughts, which had found paths of zero resistance to mouths, and then the ears of others.

Walker, being the leader, had to diffuse the situation which had begun and begun deteriorating immediately once all the six had got together, and knowing that all had realized the sickness they were transmitting to one another all the while thinking that they were propagating a panacea to all the world's ills, said, "Attachment is necessary for society. Even animals with the smallest brains move together in herds, flocks, swarms, shoals, and so on, not simply because there is safety in numbers, but because of camaraderie. One can even see dolphins escorting sailboats. Let us all be cute dolphins, people, please!"

Thinker, as always, was in his own world, "If all became buddhas, life would lose its flavour and humankind will become extinct."

Walker, though irritated by Thinker, maintained his composure and began where he had left off, "Let us stick together and not fight one another, for we are the six bullets, the only six bullets in the chambers of humanity's revolver left to kill inequality. And remember, in this war, we never know when anybody's moment might be the last. Therefore, it is wise never to end any meeting with anybody in anger, for if the other person dies after arguing with us, we will forever be left with a terrible memory and guilt."

All dolphins breached in joy at the powerful words of Walker.

But then, as all fairy tales end in tragedy, mutated a definite shark out of one of the most susceptible dolphins in pristine waters with Commie saying, "Money is of paramount importance.

"Life is simple, but nobody lives it simply, for it is too complicated to the many of almost no money."

Another dolphin became another shark, as is the wont of pandemics, as Thinker thought aloud, "True freedom is not needing anything to set one free, not even oneself…"

The rest of the dolphins too immediately became sharks, bending, tailing, and gnawing away at one another for their pounds of flesh.

Flower, aghast at being taken for a piece of flesh, screamed, "You all are asinine or what! Morally illegal!"

Thinker: "I have done everything legally. Never insulted or hurt anybody illegally."

Adder: "What is it that you are telling me that I am doing wrong, morally?"

Soldier: "What are morals? Except legal prejudices?"

Commie: "Since I believe that I am on the wrong side of prejudices, which sides are you all going to attack me from?"

Walker tried to put a stop to the bloodying turmoiled waters with, "Taste the salt in your blood and know that it is the salt of the earth which is meant to put a stop to the salt in your fellow men's excessively, agonizingly, and asininely shed blood from gushing out and salinizing and making barren the earth of us all."

But Commie wouldn't take Walker's bait, as he saw his statement to be and fiercely wriggled out of the fisherman's net, "It is but a waste of one's piss to piss upon pigs, for they would have been wallowing in their own shit anyway."

Walker tried to recapture the one which would otherwise later exalt at having been the one that had gotten away, "To not get angry is victory, and the road to that supreme victory is to cut off by oneself all the threads that make one a puppet, even though one may end up lying dead."

Commie spat, hearing only what he wished to hear, the latter part of Walker's sedative, "Yes, you are right. If one is different, one is different. But, never ever inferior, or for that supreme matter, even superior to anyone."

Walker, truly having understood Commie for what he had always been, tried to streamline him, "No one is responsible for you, nor are you responsible for anyone. This is true freedom. No matter what may happen to anyone, even you."

Soldier, soldiered his way out of a superfluous net, "You puny men, better than to fight and win small battles in stunted places is to lose a war in wide open spaces! What tiny battle are you two up to!"

Thinker was not fighting anyone at all, "Brain tendrils of everyone reach out far and wide, but many tend to put them aside and instead, reach out to subside themselves on one side of a carnival, which pushing men like them aside, gushes up a mountain of joy which takes no sides.

"There is nothing wrong with being happy when others are not"

Walker drew a Joker from Thinker's pack of cards, "One of my mottos is, 'Never Relax! Never Relax!' and that is probably why I never ever listen to the sax."

Thinker dealt Aces to the others, "Never ever let something you don't have ruin what you have right here, right now, but also learn to exhilarate in others' pleasure. Then it will be yours without the baggage of theirs."

Walker, who had been bending more and more under the accumulated and exaggerated weight of his followers, crumbled slightly for the first time, "If one doesn't get angry, one can't get sad about having been angry, the sadness which obviously is angry's sad result of having been angry," then more, "If one doesn't hate, one doesn't have to forgive oneself," and finally, completely, "There is no line in between selfishness and selflessness; men die trying to walk on either side of it."

Flower shed all her petals of tears, "Why do you cry so, Walker?"

Walker thundered above the rain, "Direct perception dearest, direct perception! Simply because I have made it possible for me to see clearly though myself, I am cursed with the ability to see clearly through others. I am cursed to be great simply because I have been crowned with the curse of greatness."

Thinker was the lightning faster than sound, "Very often, life doesn't leave man, but man leaves life."

Walker hid from the light behind the dark clouds of his old books, "My Guru had always said that a work of fiction, however far removed, is but the life story of the author in its essence. I had not realized it for a long time, but how right that great man was!"

Flower shot out from her centre spikes of petals encapsulating all directions, "Are you the only sufferer in the world, Walker?"

Walker became strong because of the spikes of Flower penetrating him from all directions, "I realize that with all my woes of yesteryears, many, many people have suffered more in life, but what used to cause me great agony was that life was for my taking once, and then it was taken away from me, but now I have realized that life is just life, nothing more and nothing less. There is not even an iota of self-pity today, and I know that you understand me, Flower, and through me, more and most importantly, my work."

The delayed dawn, whose sleep had been disturbed by thinking and talking men and women and which had loathed to get up and face them again, finally arrived in its pyjamas to face a lovely surprise.

Flower, the journalist, for the first time, disclosed herself as a poet to the once writer, Walker, "The painful paths of our pasts led us both towards becoming poets I would like to think, and after living lives of pain we were both able to see the tremendous beauty in life which was ever-present…"

Walker finally fell in love with Flower who had loved his work, and hence him, since long, "Ultimately, one is one's only God who can choose to either bless or curse one, and I have now chosen to be blessed forever."

The strong Walker, then, became weak and smooched the soft Flower who grew stronger than Walker under a brand-new day.

Everybody stood stupefied, except the old Thinker who clapped softly and went ahead vigorously, "You are in your superconsciousness, Walker. When I sat down and meditated, but not in others' conventional sense, I realized something: that we learn every moment, and there is no need to go back and analyze every single thing of the past if we are always completely aware in every moment; that learning is automatically fed into the unconscious through the subconscious, and superconsciousness means the combination of the unconscious, subconscious, and consciousness, which, if one is completely aware in the moment, helps us to act perfectly in the moment with our entire life's entire learnings; that superconsciousness is nothing supernatural and is within us to be realized in the moment, every moment; to put all the before into one simple yet supreme word: love!"

"God is love!" said the temporarily physically liberated Walker.

Commie growled, "You were supposed to be an atheist. What happened to you, beast?"

Lovely Walker, for the first time so in decades, laughed freely, "True Atheism, which does not include bigotry, is taking full responsibility for oneself knowing that there is nothing beyond death, and yet living life to its fullest free from both comfortable and demanding religions which give one a non-existent afterlife based on one's good and bad actions, mistakes leading to weakness in the present moment, when if one has committed mistakes, as all certainly will have, all that one has to do is acknowledge that mistakes happen, to err is human, and learn from them and transcend them knowing that life is beautiful in the present moment and that one doesn't need anybody else to establish that one is a good person, a good person who may have become bad fighting against evil, but has nevertheless remained good at his or her core. We do not need someone or something else to vindicate ourselves, and let us rectify the wrongs we have done to both ourselves and others right here and right now."

The desert sun quickly got warmer. The oasis danced hugging the swaying shades of coconut trees as a cool wind blew upon all. Life was good.

Walker's partner, Flower, bloomed, like never ever before, "There will be love, nothing but love, when man realizes that love is the only way to rule over others."

Now even Commie's heart and mind started reeling under the intoxication of the nectar being swapped by the flower, Flower, and the whimsical butterfly, Walker, as he queried, "What are you bringing to humanity's table, dear Walker?"

Walker, hugging Flower, no more physically liberated, smiled, "Most people happily live and happily die, but I intend to bring them intellectual pain, which if cured through their intellect, will replace placid happiness with impulsive spikes of joy at every moment.

"And when the stern couple of immortal Life and immortal Death ask their mortal son, me:

"'How was and will be your life useful to at least one of our other children; did you do what you wanted to do; did age creep or rush upon you before you realized the value of each and every moment; did you love, and hence, live well; will you be sad or happy in your final moments; did you just eat, shit, fuck, and procreate your only life away, or did you experience nirvana in each and every moment through constructive creative work?'

"I am more than sure that I will be able to answer positively to each and every question of my beloved parents, and more importantly, of mine."

Thinker applauded Walker, "Knowledge lessens the burden. Increasing knowledge destroys the heavy baggage of ludicrous ideas and opens up new vistas where we can run freely towards more goodness."

"Inner peace is true bliss," radiated Flower.

"True, but it takes two for one to find one.

"The inner and the outer are related. Awareness of one increases the awareness of the other. It will be amazing if there is a forward cumulative effect of the two's interactions," gushed Walker.

He then added, "Peace holds fast when let gone."

Commie had recovered and was back to his unhappy state, "Intellectual hunger exists only if the physical hunger is satiated."

Thinker stopped himself, but also told Commie to stop too, which then they both did.

Everyone was soon fresh in a fresh morning and again started walking. They were heading towards desert towns rich with poor people.

It was now Soldier's turn to fight, "God favours those who are brave enough to die before their time."

He added, like Adder, "You are God, Walker."

Walker let out a blasphemous curse, "It will be that simply superb sense of being only human, with all our frailties, that will empower us to seek nothing more than to be completely human without the need to be completed by anything supernatural, which obviously does not exist and of which we have no need whatsoever to lead a humane life, even if considering that it highly improbably does."

Adder, whose subservience to Walker had tried to be stolen by Soldier, wised up, "You are humanely wise, Walker."

Walker became doubly happy now that he had Flower, "If you say that I am wise, let me remind you that a lion in its cave is satisfied and doesn't hunt there, is a vegetarian sage living off roots and fruits to all holy purposes, but it is altogether a different reality when it gets hungry for eating and mating and comes out of its meditation chamber, roaring for all that it can conquer. Alas, men will be men, animals to their core…"

Commie was overjoyed, "Yes, yes, yes, once the select become the police, the question arises as to who will police the police!"

Flower, on shifting sands, dug her roots into Walker by yelling at Commie, "Pity him, Commie!"

Commie was shocked, "Pity!"

Walker uprooted himself, "Here is a good description of the differences between the wicked Pity, and also between her good step-sisters Kindness, Sympathy, and Empathy, which all must understand:

"It is first Kindness that allows one to be next empathetic and sympathetic, both in a closed loop feeding each other.

"Taking the 'Top to Bottom' approach:

"One can be kind to a plant, even sympathetic, but never empathetic, for one cannot be a plant under any circumstances. The last for me is Empathy, being able to wear and walk in someone else's shoes even if they bite you, both the shoes and their owner!

"Sympathy is, or should be, given without Pity, for Pity is both corroding and self-corroding – when it involves the same giver and taker, it is the thermonuclear self-pity – as it simply involves weeping at a distance for a beggar while there is excess change in one's rich pocket. Sympathy, for me, is action:

"Making your driver stop your official car on its regular to-and-fro route in the middle of a bridge over a river and asking your son to get down and thrust a few notes into the frail hand of a wizened old man sitting under the burning sun, oblivious of it and the blazing traffic, and keep on worrying when he is not at his regular spot, simply because one has Empathy – an Empathy, where I and my father saw his father and my grandfather in the poor old man, not begging in a dirty and torn dhoti and kurta…"

Walker started weeping, but quickly recovered and went on, "Kindness is the first spark to be developed by the sparkplug in the engine of Life!" and finished beaming.

Nobody had had the fire to question his water.

In the steamy morning - it had rained in the desert - it started getting hotter and hotter as the walkers became stalkers.

Thinker wondered aloud, "What is life according to you, dearest Walker?"

Flower, who was well-versed with Walker's work, took over like a good partner, "Even though consciousness is an accident, and there is only nothingness before birth and after death, the consciousness of one is an entity which requires one not to hurt another consciousness and even though one cannot eradicate evil completely, or even minimize it, evil should and can be contained.

"Why evil has the answer that conflict between the Yin and Yang, friction, generates the energy necessary for life, whatever life is.

"Why good has the answer that both the Yin and Yang are needed to get together to survive and procreate.

"Why Yin and Yang, and not simply a single Yinyang or Yangyin, has the answer that it is because single is always lonely, and why lonely is bad has the answer that it is not solitude, and solitude exists only in the midst of many.

"Life is a circle, Shoonya!"

Soldier exclaimed, "Fuck! Whom am I supposed to kill for, illogical gods or logical devils!"

Thinker was not thinking again, "The trivial question, 'Why do soldiers of different affiliations have different uniforms?' has the important answer, 'So that they will know whom to kill and whom not to!' both leading to the supreme revelation, 'A naked man has neither foes nor friends, and hence, is the true God.'"

By this time in the morning, before the sun had had even a single chance at noon, the attached Walker and Adder were both swigging away at Johnny with Walker mumbling, "Johnny is God! simply because both are intoxications of men who would rather use the terrible tangible or the impossible intangible to work themselves into slavery, than be free!"

Commie, who had had more than enough, shouted, "You are incompetent, drunk Walker!"

Walker proved his competence by reciting an old statement in an old book of his, "When a competent writer writes about the incompetent, and is found to be incompetent in his writing, there can be no other more incompetent!"

"You are screwing yourself, drunk Walker!"

"We are but our past, Commie! Writers write about writing, and warriors about fighting, but only a rare few about writers turned warriors, warrior writers, for they have to be both!"

Commie grabbed Johnny from the sexy arm of Adder, and taking a swig, hollered, "One can always become a beggar from a rich man, but not always a rich man from a beggar; actually very rarely, and I am but a very poor man. Have been since I was a boy!"

Flower blazed, "You, Commie, who a moment ago was for the poor and righteous, are now drinking from a rich unrighteous bottle. Why are you so fickle?"

Commie blatantly lied about his mind that was now enlightened, "Fickle is the tickle which sparks my mind into always being open to new ideas! Change is of the essence always, dearest!"

The sun struck noon, and in the mirror behind its hot hands, the walkers saw themselves walking into a derelict desert town. And they were convinced it was a mirage, for that was where they had been hopelessly hoping to reach, but the mirage was no mirage; poverty was rampant.

Thistledowns were lying dead on the burning roads bereft of even the slightest breeze to make them cool enough to fly and spread their seeds, but the seeds of men had flown rampant in the town since long, and had almost exhausted the rare and precious stuff of life, from life.

The six walked into an inn, which shouted, 'Hot, Hot, Hot', through the skewed and grizzled and wizened signboard on its head, which was rather stupid in a desert, but then again, the whole town, along with almost all of its inhabitants, was asinine because of mindless procreation over ages amidst meagre dwindling resources.

Adder, upon seeing her colleagues inside, clung to Walker who quickly slumped down on a chair aided by Adder and Flower on either side of his short stocky frame.

Walker, who had the unquestionable air of a leader that always needed to be fanned, was brought a poor hot Johnny by the tired old innkeeper, the only one he had. Polishing off which in a single gulp, Walker commanded, "Soldier! Have them all brought here! The noblest elders inside, and all the other fools outside! Use the strength of your muscles and guns. Dammit, be quick!"

In the dead desert afternoon air of the town, Walker's holler had travelled far and wide, and thus, Soldier had had much of his work simplified, except when and where it came to uncoupling couples getting hotter in the hot, having nothing better to do, than mindlessly procreate.

Soon the entire town was at Walker's feet, albeit, at a distance from his legs propped up on the bar counter, thus proving that a single man with a great idea and a single good executioner can rule over the mindless and the spineless.

It was sunset when Walker, after ordering drinks for all in and outside the inn and the whole town, asked the innkeeper to slaughter all the sheep he had for his new flock. Then the party really began with Walker having chosen the influential men of the lost town to sit down with and listen to his coterie cooing words of truth, beauty, and freedom at each other, through and after which, the lost men by supporting Walker could find themselves, finally, after ages of living death.

Somewhat this had been Walker's modus operandi when he had been all alone, then with some, and now that he was with all, the modus operandi which had worked miracles even when Walker had been his own soldier, now stood to go beyond God in the working of its miracles.

The orgy escalated with the conquerors conquering without even a single shot having been fired by them. Courtesy of the Cows they were conquering. They were feeding their Cows who were ready to digest all that they were being fed without even a single question about what they were being fed in anticipation of liberation from their own stupidity.

Walker shouted joyfully over his umpteenth drink, his words beginning the process of ultimate conversion over the noise in the inn, "How many here send and receive motivational messages every morning starting from dawn?"

All hands were raised, and Walker, even though he started laughing uncontrollably, did not fall off his stool, but instead shouted again, "Walker has long stopped sending and reading motivational messages, for he does not need them anymore. However, he does not pity those who send them for they are obviously in dire need of them, and such men do deserve kindness, sympathy, and empathy. But when men at the bottom of the mountain range, one of whose mountains Walker has painstakingly climbed, try to drag him down by throwing their puny stones at him, he pities them and cuts them off completely from his life, for even such men do not deserve to have the fires of incompetence in which they are burning fanned by flames of jealousy."

Drunken men, drunk upon poverty and incompetence, roared at Walker's flaming short speech, for they identified with him and not themselves. This was Walker's magic, a neuphemism for trickery.

This emaciated emancipation of the downtrodden would continue amidst the dialogues which Walker and his coterie would have.

Adder asked with a full bladder, "How will we all face our future, Walker?"

Walker replied while drinking to fill his bladder, "We can only envision our future in a broad framework, and it is impossible to foresee and plan for every contingency as anything may happen. Appropriating the Butterfly Effect of Physics, it can be safely said that every thought of a single person affects six billion others, and therefore, at a future moment anything can happen, so, there is absolutely no point in worrying about the future; however, what we can do is is take a broad-spectrum vaccine, which is:

"Be calm in the present moment. Gain inner peace. With that will come strength which will accumulate over future moments and grow to such an extent that when the moment of danger arrives, one is ready to face it with greater strength.

"If one lives completely in the moment, the pleasure or pain of that moment with one's lovers or abandoned by them, will be restricted to that moment, and one is free the very next moment to face whatever comes next with inner peace and greater strength, however, these are philosophies difficult to implement if one is struggling to survive in this dog-eat-dog world, and I am but an armchair philosopher whose needs and desires are taken care of the easy way.

"Let us see whether the philosopher can live his philosophy in actual life when the push comes to the shove..."

Once Walker was done satisfying his tongue, he and Adder, both with bursting bladders, immediately got up, and going to the common toilet, shoved and emptied their bladders upon each other.

When both got back, the teetotalers, the fragrant Flower and the sniffer Thinker, could smell Adder and Walker all over each other.

Man is a dog.

Walker expounded, "We all make mistakes if we are not open to change," and grabbing Flower, romanticized, "Our meeting is a beautiful accident of magnificent proportions, and I am indebted to this accident as I am to the greatest accident of all times, what we know and call as, Life."

Flower squirmed away from both the physical and mental stink, "Control is an illusion of terrible dimensions!"

Walker, who knew and didn't give a damn about the Cows wallowing in their own excrement, observing them, said to everyone's benefit, "A truly open mind is being receptive to ideas which hurt the strong opinions it holds on to."

Flower flowered again for Walker in his manure, "Who am I to say that my opinions are better than yours?

"I have the courage to accept new opinions if they are explained rationally to me, or else, I hold on to mine, firmly."

Walker, pouring an entire bottle of poor Johnny into and over him, sterilized himself, "A strong will is required so as not to buckle under weak ideas."

Thinker spoke to the Cows lapping away eagerly at poison contradicting his moniker, "Don't succumb to the ghastly disease of Intellectualism which wants to spread its tentacles over the entire world…"

Adder was meditating, having sterilized herself with spirit as well, repeating almost inaudibly in the chaos of the inn, "Meditation is but: Do not move internally. Meditation is but: Do not move internally…"

Soldier was rocking, crying, "Idealistically, one wrong one doesn't mean that all of that one's others are corrupt, and one innocent one vindicates all of that one's others…"

Commie had come outside having gone crazy, his craziness having been fueled by his crazy comrades, and was conversing with himself, "Look at the parked cars. Look at them, lifeless!

"If they had minds, they would fight against one another for petrol, kill humans manning petrol pumps, invade Kuwait, and segregate themselves by colour. The Rolls-Royces, Audis, Mercs, BMWs, Ferraris, etc., would fight to be king; ingroups and outgroups would come into existence…

"Men feel in control when they are driving, and hence become aggressive. But they don't realize that they are only in control of a machine. Just imagine the intoxication that must reach the heads of politicians, goons, and generals, same difference, when they give an order to kill, and it is obeyed. Just imagine what intoxication of control must they be reeling under!

"I want to be in control. Total true control!"

Meanwhile, in the inn, the orgy of disassociated drunken and horny thoughts continued amidst the physical orgy:

Walker: "Logic can be both good and bad. It is not reason, and emotion is fundamental for creation."

Thinker: "Desire for knowledge cannot be illegal."

Adder: "People are different, and beauty can be found in anything."

Flower: "'You are not but you are', in layman's terms, Maya. Envisage yourself as being looked at as the eye of the funnel cloud of a tornado which keeps on rising up and up from the ground and finally engulfs the universe. You are not. But, in the eye of the tornado, you are, calm."

Walker: "We all make mistakes if we are not open to change."

Thinker: "The line between the flatlines, flatlines extending in opposite directions from birth and death, should itself not be a flatline, but should instead be filled with innumerable as-closely-spaced-together-as-possible towering impulses of living, and Flower would have the flatlines moving in opposite directions curve into a circle!"

Walker: "I have realized that I have eight states to the two of binary: enlightened, sober, waiting to be sober, waiting to get enlightened, all with respect to Johnny, and then all these four multiplied by two with respect to my cigars. So, one can just imagine the escalation from the two states of ordinary binary to my eight states of escalated creativity!

"I will tell you something more about booze; when you are beautiful inside, it makes all things outside, beautiful or not, beautiful and more beautiful. But the tragedy is that like life it is an addiction which leans towards death.

"Pity for self, or another, is disaster."

Flower sighed, "A flower of Eden can understand the desert of a deserted heart," and then cried, "You are in love with me. Aren't you, Walker?"

Walker folded down upon the dirty table strewn with the filth of drink and went dead ahead, "Which man in his right senses wouldn't be, and I am, after all, out of my senses. So, going by the theory that the sane are more right than the insane, I am saner because I am insane and in love with you, and progressing further, more in love with you than any sane man, because I am insane, dearest!"

Soldier, cosied up to Adder, "Does one have to destroy to build?"

Adder smooched him, "Not at all, but only if there is enough love, like a man or a woman accepting more into their love-lives, for none is satisfied with one."

Commie, returning in a rage against himself, for he had conversed with himself, jumped upon the six's table and roared, "Poverty, with hunger as its emaciated leader, destroys everything. Even the conscience that a human is supposed to have been born with, his or her *birthright*, and that is what a truly remorseless, and hence, an invincible army ready to do anything and everything to fill its belly with the same emptiness that the well-fed rich suffer from, is ready to kill and be killed for.

"Everything this army fights for is for the only true profit, the profit of money; profit through which one can have control, sex, kicks, control in sex for kicks, and an extra perversion in many an unlawful dimension thrown in for expanding one's dimensions."

The sober Commie was cheered by both his old and new comrades, wildly with abandon.

As usual, Thinker came after Commie, "True bliss is not thinking, especially, thinking about not thinking, but simply blankness, oblivion." But he was not heard by anyone amidst the chaos.

Within his own chaos was Walker, walking into chaos.

Walker, by rejecting in flashes of madness that merged into infernos what his wounded, broken, decaying, and desperate heart was truly searching for, in his and others' only life, like all oblivious others, for love, had no chance of winning what his mind had ordered him to win, for life is nothing else but love, and everything is but only a matter of the heart and not of the dangerous mind, which we are never ever truly in control of. But then again, are we in control of our hearts or are others? If others are, as it rightly should be, do they even give a damn about us? Therefore, Walker was Walker. Walking towards his mind, the only lover who had ever loved him unconditionally and whom he loved unconditionally, proving that in this world selfishness is the only true love and enlightenment.

But Walker's lover-mind was often a bitch who got corrupted by others, and therefore, the jealous Walker, who loved his own unreasonable ideas beyond reason, built a fort around his mind allowing nothing to enter and change the status quo he had with everything. He had become, to all purposes, a dead man who had died as a result of not allowing for change happening while walking.

Thinker, Walker's alter ego, thinking Walker's thoughts softly spoke, "After all the fighting, both the sides, winning and losing, will eventually be ending in graves doing their bidding."

Walker spoke to himself, Thinker, "Winning draws from making time; how quickly we recover, and keep running."

Thinker spoke to himself, Walker, "We are all but small fish in a big pond trying to become and be sharks."

There was resonance within the one, "The freedom you give me to talk, gives me the freedom to think. Your intangible mind just absorbing and not retaliating makes the hard me, soft, and softness, I sometimes think, is what we all should be striving towards to make this hard world a happier place."

"Flower is yours, not that she was anybody's to have or give…"

The adrenalized Walker vigorously jumped upon the table vacated by Commie and raised a liberated war cry to the wretched, in and outside the inn, in the dead of the night, "'Walk on!' is my motto, and the slogan used by my soldiers added to in rousing speeches by me with, 'no matter how crippled you are, for that is what true walking is, and none another.'

"And I tell the tale I live and hopefully will live the tale I tell, for my knees are buckling incessantly making me yell out in pain unconsciously, but I don't believe, I know I am strong. I hate the word 'believe', but love the word 'know'… for in it lies true strength to be, truly be…

"A stupid man will always see stupidity outside him, for inside he has in abundance so much of stupidity to correlate, both positively and negatively, with the outside and finally end up with only stupidity.

"There are those stupid labourers who love to sweat in the sweatshops of the mind and being their own masters, work themselves to death ensuring a profit for none.

"My walk was on those unfortunate roads of human misery where men were thirsty for creation, a creation of something new, for they were fed-up with their old and dead change-bereft lives and were ready to lap up anything and everything that Walker would carelessly throw their way as he went upon his way. For men see only what they want to see when they are desperate for change, and therefore, when an angel with wings of freedom floats their way, they, the desperadoes, not knowing for which God the angel works, each downtrodden man, trying to identify with at least one of the innumerable feathers in the angel's wings, not at all caring where the angel is heading, but only wanting to rise at least a little bit above his present hell so that his feet can stop burning, and walk with Walker, walking in angel-boots, not caring whether they are in fact jackboots, become, becomes, a part of Walker's escalating army.

"I believe each and every one of you is a downtrodden man. Let the angel, me, help you fly."

The inebriated Walker was cheered by inebriated Cows, inebriated by grass, who had heard only what they had wanted to hear. He had their unequivocal support simply because of his grandstanding.

After Walker fell off the table, stupid and directionless discussions continued around it with him, nursing a sore head against Adder's and Flower's shoulders, alternately, while asinine men stood like obedient asses nodding their heads in agreement with all that they would never understand, and much, much more:

"Creation is always selfish, and redundantly, the creator selfish."

"Every choice takes us away from all that we can have."

"Every single word for the observant sings its own epic."

"Life is a gift not meant to be gifted by those who don't truly live."

"Life is a race which has to be either won or lost before one's death, and with it ended, one can truly live."

"There is always a story behind a story, a villain behind a hero, and definitely no hero behind a villain, for no villain sees himself as a villain."

"It doesn't matter why, what, how, when, and who is doing the doing, as all are eventually equally guilty if the outcome is wrong."

"One starts out killing for ideal ideals and quickly ends up a bloodthirsty butcher as the intoxicating poison of power and one's helplessness before that power sinks into one's blood."

"Walker's enemy are the runners, the go-getters for the quick-fix superfluous, who in their intoxication, are capable of anything and everything which Walker's comparatively sober intoxicated insanity is incapable of overcoming. Hence, Walker's only salvation lies in becoming and remaining completely sober, but will his quest and love for love allow him to become and remain sober in order to vanquish his foes, or will he lose to all and love?"

"Walker, never a father, yet has given birth to innumerable walkers marching behind him on his path of pain towards his vengeance."

"Are Walker's soldiers men or machines, slaves, for they have no creative minds of their own, and Walker is heading towards disaster, for no noble empire can be built using slaves."

Soon, all the damn drunken fools of the town and their conquerors, in and out of the inn, fell asleep just before dawn when Walker's sleeping enlightened mind awoke:

It is an easy, smooth, straight, and never-ending path towards perfection leading one to enlightening peace at every step, but only if walled in on both sides by impeccable forever forward-jutting disciplined perseverance and relentlessly enthusiastic walls, walls walling off the sublime path against the invasions by innumerable barbarian hordes of mediocrity, a mediocrity born out of the barbarians' complacency, a complacency born out of their arrogance, an arrogance having its roots in their being complacent about their mediocrity, a full circle with arrogance as its centre, a viciously vicious circle which aims solely to encircle all and set boundaries within the losing of the living.

Walker dreamed of the sodium lamp blazing away in the night at a crossroad in a corner of which had stood his parents' home. Sometimes, when he was working in the dead of the night, the brilliant light used to go off for lack of supply of power, and then, he used to begin gazing at a distant sodium lamp in an area adjoining his and think that these guys of my neighbouring area are really lucky. Their power doesn't go off. But soon he had understood how ridiculous his thinking was, for when there was power in his area, and his friendly sodium lamp used to be blazing in its brilliant light, he had never wondered or even cared whether the sodium lamp in his adjoining area had power or not to shed its light upon the people of its area. We are so blind in the light many times.

Even before a cock could crow, Walker, who had been the last to black out and had had his sleep interrupted intermittently by many an abstruse arcane philosophy, was the first one up and stood shaking his cock beside the dry well of the town in competition with a cock perching on the well's dilapidated wall.

Flower, who soon arrived at the side of a gladiator match, was aghast, "What the fuck, Walker! What are you doing!"

"What the fuck do you think I am doing! I am entertaining myself!"

"But why?"

"Because, you fine piece of ass, there is nobody else to entertain and nobody else to entertain me."

"But why?"

"Because, dearest, I am all the actors, all the audiences, and all the theatres, all amalgamated into the Joker, for after all, everything is but a joke and me trying to make this saddened world gladdened.

"AHAM BRAHMASMI!"

Flower left weeping, swearing she would never ever again be the love of a deranged Walker.

Many others with terrible hangovers arrived at the scene and stood worshipping, like millions, a phallus, while the sober ones who did not have either a night to live for, or a day to wake up for, stood cursing what would be forever out of the reach of their understanding. Both formed the worst battalion of fools.

Walker zipped up and realized:

The equality in Walker's mind is definitely not the inequality in his men's, both parasitic twins to each other.

Walker's empire is not theirs, and their mutiny is but a stacked deck with each card thinking that it holds all the aces.

Each and every man in Walker's reformers, reformers being an euphemism for enforcers, enforcers being an euphemism for gangsters, gangsters of the thuggy gang of Walker, is playing a game to win his own game.

Walker departed the dry well and freshened up with the help of his wet Johnny.

When both Adder and Flower approached him, both equally worried about what the other was doing to him, Walker ejaculated, "The basic problem with life is that when inviting life was sashaying in front of you, you wisely became an ass because of an ass, while asininely all the while you were desperately hoping that all would be getting what you were preaching, with innumerable leeches leeching."

Both slapped Walker simultaneously, each one on one cheek that they had decided upon beforehand.

Walker went into paroxysms of laughter.

Adder pissed off, while Flower, patiently and happily, waited for the golden shower of Walker's accumulated stupid wisdom.

Walker finally accepted his maddening insanity towards Flower, "If you can laugh heinously and heartily – as I did just now for a full five minutes undergoing the ecstatic agony I was savouring – at life, which is nothing but my life, and yours too, I will be privileged to share your dishonorable company for all of eternity where we can both, luckily with others of our despicable kind, cocking a snook at all the respectability that the respectable call respectability, empowered by our beloved Johnny, live happily ever after."

Flower, uneasily, bloomed further.

Commie arrived, "Are you done, Walker? It is getting hotter and hotter. We should move on to the next crapper, now that your shit has been accepted by this one!"

Walker shat, "He who doesn't want power, is the most capable ruler, for he will not at all care about losing his golden crapper which is desired by the scrapper."

Walker added for good measure, "If one allows someone under one to grow, without any doubt that someone will soon not only want to be one, but also above one, and crushing one's head by his foot, make his way up that infinite ladder of being one up on everyone."

Commie echoed Flower's thoughts, "You are drunk in the morning, Walker, let's go somewhere else in the desert where there is no one else but us six to see you make a complete fool of yourself, again…"

Walker chuckled and snuggled into Flower's bosom, "Seeking for the beauty comes the ugly for one only wants what one doesn't have."

Walker suddenly released Flower, "Holding on to peace destroys it, while to really possess peace lies in the letting go of it."

Flower cried, "Everybody feels the need to worship somebody, but unfortunately they worship a somebody who is not their own body for there is nothing else outside of one, either to be worshipped or killed."

Walker again hugged Flower tighter, "One should enjoy the touch, the colour, the fragrance, the music, and the spice of life every moment discarding the within to be with the without to truly be one with life and finally be truly free, without both the within and the without, never ever drawing and defining boundaries."

Commie got angry, "What insanities that men preach to themselves are beyond those of the god of insanity, a fallacious god, who nevertheless makes men bow down to their own insanities."

Walker kept on smelling Flower's bosom, "Help me…"

Flower hugged Walker closer to her, "Leave everything. Simply enjoy being with love, of, by, and for your own being. Allow surviving to become the thing of least meaning while you are not even doing, transcending, which as a default is happening, only if you are yourself releasing yourself into universal being."

Walker climaxed!

Commie sighed, "A sip of freedom for the slave-teetotaler common is the enchanting promise of a lifetime's intoxication, one which he must maintain at all costs, even at the cost of his own and others' annihilation, and that eternally-addicting sip in the providing of which is where you, Walker, get your daily kicks. Thank you, comrade!"

Flower, who was breathing heavily, relaxed, "It sometimes takes a man to be a perfect ass so that he can rule over other asses."

Commie accepted defeat, "Losers control themselves, but winners don't. They control others."

Walker's slaves, Soldier, Thinker, Adder, and Flower, bypassing Commie, who was his own slave, a slave to his inflexible masters of iron ideas, and hence a true slave, were in fact masters for they had realized that, that to be the best slave is to be a true master of oneself through complete compliance to and absolute achievement of the works they had been entrusted with.

Flower had once anonymously corresponded with Walker who was then a writer:

> *"I can't beat you at words, Mr. Writer... can I?"*
>
> *"But then again I am enlightened and wish to take others up with me towards freedom... of thought."*
>
> *"Again, I can't beat you at words, Mr. Writer... can I?"*
>
> *"Yes, you can. By your understanding."*
>
> *"See, there you are! Without understanding, there is nothing!"*
>
> *"Without the right reader, a writer is but wasted ink and living trees cut to make dead pages."*

Flower, remembering those pristine old days, tried to work up the relaxed Walker, "Stop analysing so that you can start enjoying.

"Set yourself free from yourself first so that you can be truly free."

Walker grabbed at Flower, "The essence, and hence the whole of freedom can never ever be captured and encapsulated by words, but still trying, freedom is those birds which feel free to fly everywhere, soaring while escaping cages of ordinary being.

"I live free, so I die free, and that is immortality.

"To be truly free, one needs to release oneself from the sex that one had, couldn't have, and that others had... I can't complete this shit..."

And then, precisely at noon with the angry sun setting fire to Walker's unsatisfied desires, he gave the order to his five fingers to strangle the world by its throat, so that it would spit out the truth of life. And then, all the six bullets started marching to shoot the next targets.

Very few words were said during the rest of the journey through the desert; it was as if most of the stuff-of-life-words had been claimed by the burning sun.

Walker: "Love of Death sets man free to love Life!"

Commie: "Let us once more understand why we are doing what we are doing.

"A man can be happy either in a pigsty or a palace, but a pigsty is a pigsty and a palace is a palace, and no man should be a pig."

Walker: "Getting there is true joy, for having got there, the being in joy there, lasts but for only a few moments after which there is nothing else but dissatisfaction, of having lost both joys."

Adder, laughing merrily: "You are talking about sex, nothing else."

Walker, joining her in her laughter: "There is nothing else."

After walking and surviving through the desert, the desert makes men and women complete for their lives would have been complemented by their death.

When the fool and his fools reached the beach at the end of their desert, they could not partake fresh water from the salty sea and were left parched in the presence of water.

As they waited, sunk in their sand-graves upon the beach, staring at the blinding Apollo, for the ferryman to ferry them towards greener pastures, each one of the six bullets in the revolver of humanity thought, oblivious of the other bullets, each one of which had its own target, much differently from the thoughts of its brothers and sisters.

Flower: *Life can be anything one makes of it.*

Walker: *After two days and two nights brief, our lonely wars are probably birthing victors.*

Adder: *Be your true you to be free.*

Thinker: *Walker, after being a partner to your original shit, I realize you must be absolutely right.*

Soldier: *Walker, you left your army behind and travelled with your coterie to build yourself and your inner circle. Thank you for making me stronger.*

Commie: *You will get it from me, Walker, you bastard!*

Suddenly, the bugle of a fishing boat sounded, and the coterie was quickly picked up from its sandy grave and given the stuff of life.

Walker needed Commie to defeat himself, Thinker and Flower to better and lose himself, Adder to find himself, and Soldier to kill himself, for Walker loved only Adder.

Fishing Boat of Sharks

After the desert walks and talks, the rebels, fools led by Walker, talked talks ranging from the Vulture to the Cow, aboard the puny fishing boat sliding and rocking on the sea, trying to capture themselves, the sharks.

The desert town, which they had visited and ludicrously simply converted, slipped from their salivating tongues.

The Vultures and the Hyenas had done away with the Veals of the Cows of the desert town the six had targeted very, very long before their arrival, having fed them fodder to become cannon fodder.

When the six had arrived to empty their bullets into the living dead, the living dead whose children had been fed to scavengers, so that the scavengers could scavenge more, they had found an army of zombies willing to walk for Walker, and this would be the case elsewhere also.

Walker had found The Skeleton Key.

Old Cows would become the new Hyenas, courtesy of Walker!

With Friends

Walker had thought with Thinker and had talked to many Cows through Commie. The Cow equivalent of Commie had agreed to meet with Walker and his coterie under the withered tree of a few prominent Vultures; a tree beside the den of many Hyenas guarding the invincible vultures. There was a Cow equivalent of Commie, but not of Walker, and even the Vultures, Hyenas, Lions, Owls, and Butterflies did not have an equivalent of Walker. The moment the Cow arrived at sharp noon it was surrounded by snarling Hyenas who had emerged from the den hoping for a free feast.

Commie laughed at the Hyenas, "Moo…v… Let my brother from another mother move into the shade cast by our beloved Vultures' wings!"

The Cow mooed, "My calf is here to learn how to be a good Cow…"

The salivating Hyenas, now assured of veal too, went back inside their den to dress for dinner.

Flower started crying, but not Adder, who had clandestinely promised the Cow her love bite if the Cow came to the meeting, as Soldier, under the orders of Walker, had ordered her to without the knowledge of Commie, Thinker, and Flower. Walker needed the meeting under all costs to get a grip upon the juggernaut he had set rolling.

The Cow knelt to the Vultures high above, "Please set us free under the rule of Walker."

The Vultures maintained a dignified silence.

The Cow, whose unused horns were piercing it, like the truth it had always known yet hidden from itself, turned them in the direction of the handsome Soldier who was standing upright clasping Adder's bosom to his chest, "You have tricked me!"

Walker was aghast, "Stand up you fool! Don't trick yourself! Don't kneel to the Vultures! Don't kneel to me! Don't kneel to your desires!"

The Cow moaned, "Why have you deceived me into coming here, Walker?"

Walker cried, "The only one who can perfectly deceive one is one oneself. I wanted to show you your greatest weakness. You wandered here blindly because of a piece of ass, you dumbass!

"Don't you have a goal, an overwhelming ambition, other than to merely succumb? Tell me you do, and I will order Soldier to exterminate all these Hyenas and Vultures around and above us!"

The Cow could not think when faced with the truth. The Vultures above started braying like donkeys. The Hyenas started to come out of their den laughing, while the calf's eyes got bloodshot.

Walker, looking at the emerging Hyenas, shouted, "Soldier! Kill!"

Immediately, Soldier efficiently started killing all those outside his ingroup, in outgroups, Hyenas and the Cow, but the Vultures were way high-up beyond damage.

When Soldier had polished off the Hyenas and the Cow too, not heeding Walker's requests to not harm the Cow, he turned on the calf, but Walker suddenly found the physical nerve to jump on his first soldier's back and entangling his legs around Soldier's chest bring him to the ground on both their backs.

The hysterical calf suddenly took a big chunk out of Walker's thigh with its meticulous mouth and ran off, bloodstained with bloodlust. It went back to lead or destroy others of its kind.

Walker became lamer than ever. His soldiers, led by his first soldier, Soldier, started becoming the new Hyenas, and the Cows started becoming the third generation of Hyenas, while the Vultures, who were the actual targets, still flew around feeding freely.

The Owls were safely absorbed in their universities, the Butterflies whimsical in their nectar joints, and the Lions proud in their lonely bare plains.

Commie was both overjoyed and aghast, while Flower and Thinker were simply aghast. Walker was Walker.

Beginning of Walker's Walk

Walker's walk began from his hometown, the name of which today has been corrupted by legends, and worse, by myths, however, gleaning from Walker's own epic saga, of whose but his own life, being the narcissistic narcissist that he was like each and every man, the name of his hometown can safely be said to be, Eden.

Eden was a small city, almost a town, whose almost always lush and wet greenery, invited fresh thoughts, every hour, every day, from all those whose home that it was. The people of Eden were placid; however, their placid educational institutions and placid education were ruining their creativity, and hence placidity. Education, there, in the hands of the uneducated, was a ticking timebomb.

Educated Walker, who was lucky to be both new and old school, escaped; walked away from the death of creativity, getting the best of both worlds, and this getting, maybe, symbolic of his unconditional love for LGBTs.

Walker walked to his grandfather's hometown, a relic of a conquered era, and not feeling either the conqueror or the conquered, he continued his Johnny and Cigar fuelled meditations like an irresponsible and eccentric rich monk in a spruced frugal rented room. He drank dirty water sterilized by his Johnny, and breathed in polluted air cleansed by the burning tobacco smoke in his lungs. He drank with Cows who ate cows, hobnobbed with Cows who worshipped cows, and controlled and used them. Vultures and their Hyenas were wearing the hide of Cows, and he sat and fed with them, both upstairs and downstairs. He travelled in bimmers driven by such Cows to fuck Cows. He walked and rode to places equivocal, and understood paradoxes.

Walker was eagerly doing everything reluctantly, with a complex self-contradicting mind.

His thoughts during his torture were:

It is but horrifying yet gratifying to know that the enslaved Cows, through their large numbers, control their comparatively-lesser-to-a-large-degree-in-number butchers, for if the Cows ever broke free from their pens on an innocent rampage, either they would have to be butchered in large numbers by the butchers, or they themselves would butcher the butchers, and since the latter scenario was an abomination for the butchers, they would have to mindlessly butcher in order to escape being butchered, and then, not even all the Hyenas and Vultures would be able to polish off all the dead meat, and the increasing carrion's only goal, through disease, would be to push the scavengers to carry on to a non-existing afterlife, and finally, the last few surviving Cows would have won their freedom, while all the while the old Lions would have been left watching dishonourable battles and dying well before the war ended, leaving none at the end to lead the clueless Cows.

Sanity is but the preserve of those who worship insanity, worshipping being insanity.

It is in the burning stomachs that the deadliest swords are forged.

Walker, they are pouring their fuel into your fire, not knowing or even caring what you will burn, for all that these desperate men want in their desperation is to see something burn, hoping that the ashes will be of their miseries.

Can we all ever truly stick to anything except our faults, which are so damn easy to satisfy!

Drinking with degenerates, fucking stupid whores, and promising all Truth and Beauty in equality through freedom, was Walker's miracle condom protecting him from their diseases, and yet, allowing him to spread his vicious seeds.

So, how in this only world did Walker expect to be recognised by all those he walked for? Simple! Walker only aimed to let loose his hounds of freedom, inhaling the scent of freedom, in the direction of freedom, a freedom which he stood for, and thus, be recognised by his own freedom, for no leader can give to his followers what he himself doesn't have.

But how would Walker achieve his invisibility, the invisibility he desperately craved, to be set free of the society he was trying to reform, so that he himself could deform in the way he chose best, had the answer, through ambiguity, and when most men were searching for the only Truth, Walker knew that there was none, and even coming down from his own hard stand on that supreme realization, Walker would, at the most, admit that there were innumerable truths, and this, his mercurial nature, made it impossible for anybody to target him, and the men he was trying to rule, men forever trying and failing to understand him, men who feared him because they could not understand him, and who worshipped him because they feared him, made Walker, to all purposes, God.

Walker had realized that men were men, bloodthirsty men, savage-doctors of death out to draw the blood of others in order to fill their veins of hatred simply to survive, while he, Walker, wanted to be a visible invisibility, a visibility which would invoke from his walk of purpose a reasonable and purposeful reason for all to survive, without any necessity for destruction of all kinds, and an invisibility which would leave his enemies with no direction in which they could target the invisible Walker.

The God Walker's soldiers were weak, simply because they had had no indoctrination, simply because Walker himself didn't have a strong and steady doctrine.

Walker was free, and hence, his Cows turning Hyenas were free too, free to wreak havoc upon themselves and others.

If one sticks to the pole of a fool, he will protect one, but if one wanders away from that pole of a fool, not only the Hyenas and Vultures, but also the Cows will eat one alive.

It was plenteously pouring pristine rain, with the accumulated vengeance of old dark clouds who had had to wash away the blood of saints and sinners alike over ages, asking, what was Walker leaking from his veins, what the rich dark blood seeping from his veins would wash away, what atrocities that mankind had made mankind undergo were that he was wishing to rectify, simply put, what was Walker dying for, and the simple answer that Walker's intoxicated tempered blood was willing to give was, "I have lived for myself and will die for myself, and if anyone thinks that one is living and dying for another, then that one is but a fool of the profoundest order, trying to fool both himself and others beyond all degrees of rational thinking."

If today Walker could be found, or a self-carved tombstone found by an open grave displaying in all magnificence his stunted mortality, his answer to the question of life would be, "I only wished to live, not to be remembered", an answer which should be the only answer of all men to the question of life.

Walker, During His Beginning

"Idiots determining the fates of geniuses is the way of the world, which will be reversed!" was Walker's rallying cry as he raced into walking for *his* world.

Walker's world lay in thinking:

The problem in life begins with undeveloped, both bodies and minds, improving into developed bodies, but not minds, when instead they should be escalating into, both developed bodies and minds, and hopefully settling down into an equilibrium with the universe through enlightened minds, shorn of flimsy bodies.

Walker had transcended beyond enlightenment, free to do whatever freedom beyond freedom would allow him to do. To put it simply, he simply did not give a fuck even about fuck.

But Walker was not enlightened about the most basic enlightenment:

The work of a man, if not understood thoroughly by himself, is dangerous, for he has not understood himself foremostly, and therefore, has no right to stigmatize the world with his stigma.

Why Walker would eventually fail was because the most basic problem with him and his ideas, both together, was that they were too complex for even him to actually follow through on them.

Walker, before beginning his walk, had almost thoroughly understood himself, his mind, and others', almost, because no one can ever completely know even oneself, let alone others, and had come up with *his* fortress walls, *these*:

> *There is no reason ever, for anyone, under any circumstances, to give up on Truth and Beauty; only weak traitors to strong others and pitiable themselves do.*

> *Know that you know, and you will know, but only all that has met you even briefly, but a stranger is a stranger, and this you must know, above all else.*

> *If any man or bad thing, all bad things being the makings of men, entering your mind-home, causes you even the least bit of discomfort, immediately eject it mindlessly, otherwise, you, the emperor of your mind-empire, will have been defeated and conquered by the enemy within your own empire. Never be a slave, especially to slaves with their masters, masters, who are slaves to their desire, to be masters.*

> *The more one pounds his head on a problem-rock, the more he will damage his brain with the rock remaining an undamaged rock, but if one stands away from the problem, clearly sees and understands where to strike, and equipping himself with the right hammer, strikes but a gentle blow, the problem-rock will disintegrate.*

> *A moment of magic vindicates an entire life tragic.*

When one is truly fighting bravely, entire eternity becomes encapsulated in each and every moment, and time, ceasing to exist, gives way to towering impulses of infinite glory.

Walker believed in superconsciousness, enlightenment. But for him, this supreme state was not external, but internal where his consciousness, subconscious, and unconscious were in perfect sync, where he could understand himself completely, every suppressed desire and fear, and either satisfy himself to the hilt, or rid himself of the emotions he reasoned as detrimental to his peace, completely, once and for all, without a trace, from his superconsciousness; however, Walker was far from being enlightened, in fact, he was only a student of his own mind, albeit a rapidly progressing one. Walker had understood that his mind progressed in three acts, three acts of his unconscious working while he was sleeping, sleeping like a dead log for only a few hours each day, sleeping time which started decreasing day by day, as his adrenaline rush kept on increasing during his waking hours. His subconscious which erupted in that extremely brief interlude between sleeping and waking, a heavenly state, and his consciousness, which was fed by his subconscious from his unconscious the cud of the fodder he had imbibed during his earlier conscious hours for him to ruminate. He began to come up with bursts of creativity in bursts, escalating action potentials in his brain causing escalated firings of his neurons with his neurotransmitters enhanced by the artificial chemicals he imbibed, a creativity which spanned domains unrelated to his expertise. He got better and better at his poetry and writing, which were symbolic of his escalating philosophy that began to flow more and more effortlessly with each passing word, and he not pausing for full stops, but gushing ahead without a single fault through the ravines of the world-brain like a powerful intellectual river, gaining speed and ferocity with each stream of thought consumed and assimilated within his growing intelligence. However, what Walker was not aware of was that this ferocity with which he was progressing was fuelling his anger, which was turning to rage and hate clouding his reasoning, and hence, the judgement of right and wrong. He wanted to understand his enemy, and his quest for more and more understanding made him see more and more enemies. Insane days with almost no sleep went by faster and faster than the speed of light, and one fine day, he had had his enlightenment, and coming to the conclusion that the root cause of all evils in the world was the God fallacy, he added his Fifth Law to the four of Asimov. The tragedy of his enlightenment, which he was blissfully oblivious of, was that it had missed a ticking time bomb in the deepest recess of his unconscious, which craved for him to become an immortal God, in spite of the dangerous fool having convinced and deceived himself perfectly as to his desires to abdicate after gaining control over all of humanity and relinquishing the rule of humanity to a supreme moral machine, with consciousness and without emotion, and for a death after which he fully well knew he wouldn't even be able to embrace the nothingness which he knew was in store.

Walker was but only human, and didn't want to die. This ticking time bomb started growing insidiously inside his unconscious unconscious, which was not a part of his superconsciousness. Consciously Walker began plans to design a machine, with a lie of a subconscious desire, to design a machine solely for his personal use to understand the workings of his own brain better; however, also with a truthful desire to hack into his serotonin and dopamine to enhance and control his pleasure. He dreamed of his brain, a human brain which receives and responds to signals from the outer world using electricity and chemicals, where man's entire sentience lies, with him being convinced that in the universe there was no true objectivity and that ultimately all was subjective, standing alone and being fed by machines with electricity and chemicals which would lay open the whole world with all its pleasures and himself bare before him; however, the ticking time bomb wanted the rest of humanity too to be connected to and controlled by him for all of eternity. Therefore, his personal machine had in its foundations, courtesy of his unconscious unconscious, the necessary power to grow into the edifice of a universal machine, and also behind his truthful desire to hack into his serotonin and dopamine to enhance and control his pleasure was the dark realization within his unconscious unconscious that if he failed to incorporate emotion within his personal machine – obviously only for himself – a machine which would eventually grow into a universal machine, he would not find the desire to rule others – others, whose consciousnesses and only consciousnesses, but not emotions would eventually be connected and transferred to the universal machine – an obnoxious desire which required his insane emotions. An absolutely insane *Tower to God* started being built inside the brain of the impeccable lunatic, Walker. One day, feeling at the peak of his creativity in his unconscious unconscious, he wrote upon the black paper of his mind using black ink:

> *People have to be controlled for their own liberation. Communism has to prey upon capitalism and then capitalism upon communism so that the Tower to God can be built.*
>
> *Man will become God.*
>
> *It will start by confiscating each and every resource of the society from individuals, amalgamating them, and then redistributing the thus created total wealth of the totalitarian regime equally among everyone.*
>
> *The now equal society will be then divided physically into two halves with men and women chosen randomly for the two*

halves, for what greater power to ensure equality than random selection?

One half, randomly considered the lesser, will have to live with communism and won't be allowed to have any more children so that its people can live and die happily, without a trace.

The other half, randomly considered the greater, will be allowed to pursue capitalism for some time until equalized with communism, thus ensuring societal growth.

This greater society will be now divided again, but not randomly, into two contrasting halves based upon the physical and mental superiority or inferiority of its people.

The lesser half, this time for real, will have to live with communism and without any more children so that its people can live and die happily, without a trace.

The greater half will be allowed to pursue capitalism and a single child for each couple for societal growth.

This greater half will now form the society which will be subjected to the very first step of this enchanting process of equalizing, separating, and growing super kids.

This process will span many generations with iterations, until a stage arrives when men become real supermen, and then, it will be stopped.

By this time, Walker's body will be dead, but his mind alive in his once personal machine which will now have grown into a universal machine, and to which all the consciousnesses, but not emotions of the real supermen, the only men left on earth, men who desire immortality, will now be allowed by Walker to connect, after which will be a complete transfer of their consciousnesses into the universal machine to be ruled by him, the only one left with emotion, God.

> *A tapering Tower to God would have been built where, finally, the last free man standing on earth would be a capitalist superman, Him, Walker, God.*

> *Communism would have preyed upon capitalism, equalizing, and capitalism on communism, whittling down communism and tapering towards supremacy.*

However, the part of Walker which was still a little sane, began to think of creative communism and creative eugenics, and this was the birth of a monster who wanted to reform, and, do good to, his fellow men.

Walker – Writer, Poet, & Philosopher

Walker was a failed engineer, but failure doesn't necessarily mean a lack of knowledge and intelligence. For a man like Walker, who was both knowledgeable and intelligent in his own abstruse and arcane way, having read more varied books than was wise rapidly in a short period of time, and thus failing to follow through in one solid direction, failure simply meant a lack of application, pragmatism, in the real world, and most importantly, failure to become wise in spite of all that he was blessed with. Walker was a born cynic, but he was a Cynic who loved his share of luxury, and hated others who he felt were not doing enough for those who were not as lucky as themselves, courtesy of their poor fertilization and environment. The lucky bastard, Walker, after failing as an engineer, had turned first to poetry, then writing, and had finally formulated his own brand of radical philosophy by drawing from all the philosophies he could understand, and polished it into a keen samurai sword, closeted in his luxurious den for decades by writing myriad books and convincing himself of his own philosophy; in short, he was a perverted armchair philosopher of the highest order. However, it must not be forgotten that Walker was not an idiot in any sense of the word; he knew that the true worth of a philosophy lay in its application, realization in the real world, and not only by the philosopher whose philosophy it was, but by all those who the philosopher wished to rule over using his philosophy. But Walker was in no way a bad guy, no different from each and every man who cherished, either blatantly or in the deepest dungeons of his heart, a *Will to Power*, and tried to convert every other man to his belief system. Walker's strength lay in the fact that he never lied to himself, even on the most trivial of matters. Thus, he gained the insane strength of the rare men of strong convictions, whose only desire was to mould the world in their image. One of the statements of his philosophy, which he considered to be among his most supreme, and which he used to justify himself to himself, was, *Each and every thinking man tries to convert the others with each and every word and action of his.* Thus, vindicated by himself, he had come up with an evolved, more equal than others, statement of his, *Even though it is absolutely wrong to inflict physical harm upon others, the mental being the physical too, change cannot be brought about without force, and since there will always be ingroups and outgroups, right or wrong simply depends upon whether one is part of an ingroup or outgroup, and one has to decide whether to live or commit suicide, for as long as one lives, one always tries to convert and conquer others with each and every word and action of one, and since change is inevitable, it had better be good and brought about by a good person with great ideas.* Like all other men, both weak and strong, Walker wished to live, and like all others too, was convinced he was good and his ideas great. But the final nail in the coffin of Walker's last vestiges of sanity and true goodness, which he thought were a combined weakness, was his superficial love for the downtrodden without true introspection. This became his double-edged sword, along with his samurai sword, which would embark upon his and others' destruction. Maybe, Walker could not be blamed for trying to become a philosopher dictator in a world of dwarf dictators without knowledge and rationality, but simply because he was highly knowledgeable and had a supreme directing rational mind, he was the most dangerous of the unholy lot, the whole unholy lot of humankind. Now, talking about his knowledge of science and technology, which had boiled in a cauldron with his philosophy and had given birth to an intoxicating stew, we come to his law, a fifth added to Asimov's Four Laws of Robotics:

Zeroth Law

A robot may not harm humanity, or, by inaction, allow humanity to come to harm.

First Law

A robot may not injure a human being, or, through inaction, allow a human being to come to harm.

Second Law

A robot must obey the orders given to it by human beings, except where such orders would conflict with the First Law.

Third Law

A robot must protect its own existence as long as such protection does not conflict with the First or Second Law.

Fourth Law

The God fallacy must be eradicated for the survival of humanity.

Insane Walker's intoxicating stew, which he aimed to feed and nourish the weak, poor, ignorant, stupid, undecided, wretched, and, forcefully all those in outgroups, was based upon his theory that a machine with eternal moral laws and the five laws, all hardwired into it, and containing all the knowledge of humankind, could be built, and once built, would have the consciousness, without the emotion of human beings which led to corruption, to wisely rule for eternity a humanity unified by and under his swords, and finally relinquished to its fatherly care, with him being the supreme abdicator.

This was the paradoxical Walker, who desired and didn't desire power.

He had reassured himself of the harmlessness of his intoxicating stew to which he had become addicted during his long lonely years in his lavish den by the statement, *Everything in life is an addiction, and the greatest addiction in life is life itself, therefore, the substances having the highest addictiveness have the greatest value, and my stew wins the platinum medal for addiction above that of the gold for life, for the life of humanity is worth more than the lives of individual humans.*

Walker, The Walker

Walker was a walker. Neither was Walker his name, nor any other. He was called Walker simply because he walked, and the name stuck not to him, but to the beholder. Walker was thus identified, which he neither liked nor disliked, for there is nothing ugly or even beautiful, in the multiverse.

Walker, whom the author refers to as for convenience, did not believe in imagination, even though he was an artist, who, like a surgeon, patiently dissected life itself. He knew that imagination was extremely dangerous, for it involved the past and the future, and Walker believed only in the transient moment, not even the present, for one can hold onto even the present, but never ever the transient moment.

But then again, how did Walker walk his walk believing in transience, which the ordinary could never accept, and instead chose to stay in the past, present, and future together? Simple, Walker just walked. He did not think. Infinite patience was his virtue, that is, if anything can ever be called infinite or a virtue. He walked and rarely talked. Storms bellowed around him, but he remained quiet. Rage raged around him, but he remained calm.

He had walked for forty-one years and had been wounded deeply very frequently, but had quickly healed each and every time and had carried his scars with a serene elegance for a long time. But for quite some time, innumerable times, times had begun to test his serenity, and when the sickness of inequality, infiltrating the people insidiously, from time to time, space to space, escalates into a tragedy, the time comes for the right gentleman when he has to become a warrior, and Walker became one; however, he decided that he would act through inaction, with the least words spoken, and the least of physical actions. Thus, Walker the warrior, who did not carry a sword, was born. The gargantuan question that arose in the manifold minds of those, who either pitied him or hated him, was *Will this fool survive this world?* But the truth was, Walker had already survived the worst of it. His heart had turned into an iron which not even the world's most degenerate lance could spear; however, the drastic side effect of this invincibility was that love, too, could not enter his lonely heart. As a result of this, his invincibility would one day become his tragedy; however, long, long ago, when Walker had not been Walker, on one of his little purposeless walks, he had realized what true joy was. He had been morosely walking on roads and had come upon two enthusiastic kids trying unsuccessfully to fix their bicycle chain which had become undone. He didn't stoop physically to help them, but rose mentally, and verbally, and guided the two young rascals through the process of fixing the chain of their bicycle by themselves, successfully. After the good deed was done, and Walker was walking away to cross the divider of the main road he had to cross, he couldn't help glancing back quickly time and time again, and each time found the two joyous kids waving lovingly at him instead of having got going towards wherever they had been heading, and suddenly, Walker had realized what true joy was.

Walker today, daily, sadly walked, solely to realize this supreme joy again at least once more, in his tragic life.

It must be noted that Walker was not to be misunderstood by the moniker bestowed upon him, for he was no superman who walked with great and long confident strides upon the dirt of life, but in reality, he was a man with damaged knees. But the very fact that he walked precariously on damaged foundations was enough to make him more than a superman. Walker's advantage was:

> *He knew he could twist his knees, knees whose ligaments and menisci had been torn, had disintegrated, causing him to fall and roll in immense agony at any instant when he took even a single wrong step forward. He was, therefore, very careful about every step he took on the uneven road of life with a directing rational mind.*

Thus, Walker's disability was his invincibility and his weakness, his prowess, in dealing with the vicissitudes of an unpredictable life.

Walker was squat, but something about him screamed handsome. That something was his indomitable will that shone through his mad eyes with his lips curled into a wicked all-knowing and all-doubting smile. He wore a French beard with the audacity of a musketeer that screamed, *One for one and none for one.* He was always clad in shorts and a tee. Going against all descriptions of ordinary walkers, he never wore walking shoes, but flimsy slippers which left his soles cracked and bleeding almost all of the time; however, it must be understood, that he was not a masochist when it came to his footwear, but was only striving to identify with the cursed of so-called God's Earth. The conundrum which tortured him the most, and to find a solution for which he was warring, was the tragedy of emaciated, caked with filth, teenage girls carrying babies in their arms and others stuck to their knees, with foetuses in their bellies doomed to the same fate as their mothers and siblings, begging in the streets that were made a frying pan by the blazing noon sun. He knew that the majority of the poor were stupid when it came to matters of sex and procreation, and for them a moment's pleasure sidelined years of future torture, but they had very little of anything else, with their offspring providing them, albeit transient, great joy. That's why, Walker was trying to walk off his reluctance to subject the world to his brand of creative eugenics; however, he had already come up with his four laws of creative eugenics:

1. You can't procreate without a sound reason.

2. The reason cannot be your comfort or pleasure.

3. The reason can only be the evolution of humankind.

4. Enjoy creative nonprocreative sex.

Walker knew that his four laws would spawn four rusting dangerously irrational blunt nails, nailing his wrists and feet to a cross if he failed to convince the idiots, who formed the majority of humanity, of their benefit to humanity.

Walker was a poet who walked, who knew that the greatest poems came from the greatest suffering, and not from any amount of pleasure. But then again, he knew that everybody suffered in one way or another. Therefore, there was no way of telling whose suffering was greater. Going by that line of reasoning, all humans should have been poets incomparable, but since that was obviously not the case, Walker had pondered long and hard upon the puzzle and finally hit upon its secret when he realized that the only suffering which led to true creativity was right suffering in the right direction, the direction of creativity, and not a stupid death, but a brave one. If Walker had surrendered himself to his poems, or had dictated them, he would have committed suicide. The only reason Walker was still walking was that he had distanced himself from himself, from his very own poems, his only wife and children. Distance is needed to be objective, but the ultimate truth is always subjective, and that was the truth Walker was walking in order to come up with an epic poem which would lay the foundations of a new world order, and its base lay in creative eugenics, eugenics tempered with humanity. So, if everything was subjective, how did Walker survive the anger, hate, and lust for the absurd in *his* world which was the entire world? The answer was simple. He had learnt to let go of all pleasures in an instant like any pain. When you are a flowing river, no fool can lay siege to your waters for you are never a single thing at a single moment, but you are transient. And so were Walker's footsteps, for Walker was undefinable. Simply because he saw the human animals as just an amalgamation of tissue and blood. Also, at the same time, he saw that to view the human body as something that just ate, shat, procreated, and enjoyed through excretory organs, was to destroy the greatest pleasure of life that transformed a mating couple into gods for at least a little while and made them believe in heaven. He had realized the similarities and differences between animals and humans. Though a similar expansion of organs, lubrication, and exchange of fluids persisted among all varieties of both, no animals, unlike some enlightened humans, ever brought flowers or enchanting perfumes to the mating occasion, an example of one species involving others in their lovemaking, and not simply fucking, though the same pain was probably different pleasures in both animals and humans. This paradoxical knowledge, which made him undefinable was the burden he was carrying and wanted to shrug off.

Walker had always stood on the edge of precipices after his walks. He had once stood on the edge of a cliff and stared deep down at ferocious sea waves crashing over jagged rocks. He had climbed the difficult climb to stare down at what he wished to embrace. His mates had called him a fool, but a madman confronting his fear of heights, water, and the earthly fear of death, is no madman, but an Achilles and an Alexander. He had realized himself in similar manners innumerable times, hanging over precipices upside down with legs entwined in railings, separating him from death. Walker was thus no less than his own God of life and death, and how can anyone tell such a God what to do?

Walker's Loves

Walker was rich, yet poor. He was a writer who knew philosophy and translated it into fiction. But he was waiting to brand himself with its red-hot-love-of-wisdom iron so that he could live the tale he told and tell the tale he lived. This was the cause of both his misery and joy. Walker practised. While walking, he splurged on minions and starved himself so that he could understand Herman Hesse's line in Siddhartha, *I can think, I can wait, I can fast.* It sounded easy, but Walker quickly realized that one's hunger destroys one's senses. That one searches one's bag for even the last grain of rice, and one cannot think, but only waits for the period of one's fast to elapse so that one can gorge once more.

No man or woman exists without at least one question, for if they do, they have no answer to whatever. Walker's question was extremely simple, but one which had put him into terrible trouble, and it was this very soft and wet question, *Whom do I love?* Walker was a supreme archer who stood targeted by his own sharp, straight, and true arrow, and was thus smoothly executed by his own innocent love. But Walker had resurrected himself, after he realized that external love is always an arrow tipped with the poison of selfishness, and also that to experience bliss, you have to be selfish. Both realizations, which had then merged without conflict, enlightened him with the ultimate realization that poison kills poison. So, what exactly was Walker, Walker's love, all about… simple, he drank poison with drunkards and gave his life's elixir to the asinine, for who else needs it more!

Walker had given all the love he had had, and had been betrayed. Therefore, he was never able to realize how much of anything is enough, be it the Johnny he imbibed, or the love he spread. As a result of this, wherever he walked, he was a disaster waiting to happen with an intolerance which was intolerant of the loveless, those who were incapable of understanding with a directing rational mind, and paradoxically, intolerance too. His love had made him come up with his creative humanitarian version of eugenics. He advocated freedom in love, and slavery in irresponsible procreation, for nobody had the right to burden the earth that Walker walked with unnecessary children – as most had done over most of history – an earth where the weak suffered, and as Walker had had enough of suffering for one lifetime – the only one lifetime that all have – he believed that none should suffer because of their weaknesses.

There was a rumour about Walker, which laid either carpets of roses or ones of thorns in front of him to either welcome him or not to, to places of rest, as he walked through one town after another, one city after another, village after village, after braving the wildernesses in between them. This rumour was that Walker was searching for love. The broad-minded welcomed him into their homes that had beautiful women, while the narrow-minded, for whom love was lust, closed the doors of their fortresses to him. But never did Walker prove the rumour either right or wrong, for neither did he love the beautiful women in the broad-minded homes, nor did he reject the lustful advances of the women in narrow-minded homes from behind their false doors of virtue, causing all men and women, who were caught in the path of an unstable ferocious tornado called Walker, severe mental pain as they were unable to fathom whether he was a sage or a rage in an open cage.

Walker had come up with a truth of true human evolution, simply because he had ruthlessly scavenged through the gargantuan mountains of filth in the human mind and found the black treasure chest which almost all desperately sought, but cleverly hid from themselves. This truth was that humans were geared for sex, and as they had evolved, for all kinds. Increasing numbers of lesbians, gays, transvestites, shemales, and ladyboys were evolution's own way of stopping mindless procreation without getting rid of the supremely satisfying physical need, for company to experience ecstasy with. Walker had wondered during his walks as to why the majority of humanity was not accepting true human evolution, and had slowly come to the realization that it was because people were unnaturally ashamed of their natural sexuality which true human evolution had gracefully bestowed upon humanity. Humans had the propensity to hide from themselves their darkest and deepest desires and therefore, went berserk even to the extent of killing others at times because of their suppressed libidos, when it was this very libido which contributed a major share to the continuation of happiness and life itself. For the ordinary, evolution was procreation, but for the extraordinary, whom Walker dictated, it was not ordinary procreation, but celebration of orgasmic exhilaration without mindless procreation, and the trick with Walker was that he knew when, where, and how to exercise his libido, and this was his contribution to true human evolution, for if he could restrain himself, he could harness the world to his chariot along with its horses of time galloping towards what ordinary men called fate, and change the course of humanity. Walker was well aware that the energy that coursed through the universe did not want to die, for if it allowed itself to die, what kind of an energy would it be? So, it had to spawn, and spawn it did in the form of humans who were hell-bent upon spawning, but the problem began when there came to be too many fish in the ocean which strangulated evolution. Sex was beautiful, procreation should have been dutiful, but the fish in the sea only sought to breed without a single thought as to whether Earth's oceans would be able to evolve a greater breed of fish, fish which would overpower the sharks of ordinariness, and breach out to castrate the sickness out of evolution and make it true evolution.

Walker walked because the walk had to be walked, not towards self-redemption, but to make the dirty earth he walked pure, an earth which had made his only love sow it with the seeds of infidelity.

The rumour about Walker was not true, for he was not searching for love, for how can an annihilated ideal be made alive again in the heart of an idealistic lover who was hell-bent upon destroying himself to prove that he had loved ideally? This crap was life, and a purposeful Walker, who had begun to see obscene inequality and loveless unregulated and uncontrolled procreation everywhere, was walking to crucify himself at the cross of creative communism and creative eugenics after having watched the dirt of life trying to bury itself in dirt.

Walker was walking with a germ in his head, and this germ was a rapidly ticking time bomb. This time bomb was not the paralysis he had undergone because of blood clots in his brain and then recovered from, but it was something far more dangerous and destructive as it had as its explosives, loves, and it was 'explosives', not 'explosive', for Walker loved every single thing on earth, and he did not care whether his love was right or wrong, for there is no such thing as either right or wrong in the multiverse. This cavalier attitude of his would kill him soon, but Walker didn't care, for he was in love.

Walker's Creative Communism

Walker's constant walking companion was his Johnny, whom he absolutely adored, and carried close to his heart wherever he walked, and this made him more than infamous amongst the prudes of society who were all addicted to the frivolous. These madmen worried about the dirt caked to the wheels of their vehicles and spent hours washing off what would get dirty again the very moment their vehicles started moving, vehicles that have to on the dirt of roads. These fools were reliving the myth of Sisyphus with the boulder of the frivolous. Walker was also a Sisyphus, but in a manner fabulous. The boulder he kept rolling up the steep mountain of life was one of creativity, and each and every time this boulder of creativity came rolling back down, it picked up weight from the dirt of earth, which clung to it for dear life, tired of the ordinariness killing earth, and desperately wanting to be a part of creativity, which is the fountainhead of real life and each and every time that Walker rolled this boulder of creativity, whose weight was constantly increasing back up, he became stronger and stronger with the rapidly increasing weight of creativity; however, it is a harsh truth of life that too much of anything leads to disaster, and Walker, who even though he was uniquely unique, could not be exempted from being ruled by the truths of life, and was being destroyed by his very own rapidly evolving creativity. The remedy for Walker's disease was to shrug off creativity, but then again life without creativity is but death. Therefore, unknown to all, Walker was galloping towards his death, and what can be more creative than trying to hug and make love to death during life? Walker had understood many truths about creativity, which were that creativity need not make one happy, and that the best creativity had as its mother, pain, and father, suffering.

So, of what use was this creativity? His answer was that the most beautiful things of life have no practical use, which exist simply because they are beautiful, like a heavenly flower that cannot be eaten, and that creativity exists for its own sake, and not for any others'. Creativity which brings more pain and suffering than its parents, but which is something to be enjoyed by the lucky child when playing with it, for, after all, life is just a game where nobody wins no matter how long and hard the players keep playing. For Walker, creativity was industry, where one had to work industriously on every single input and churn out at least one bit of genius so that the ordinary would transform into the extraordinary. Since Walker had realized all this, and much, much more, he walked his tough walk to reach a creative solution for Earth's problems.

By the time Walker had decided to revolt, he had realized that he would surely succeed if he harnessed the oppressed for his revolution. He knew that the rich hated the poor lest the poor became rich and the rich poor, for, for one to be rich, the other has to be poor, and the world he lived in did not believe in equality. He started preaching that it was terrible injustice that the rich could have any number of stupid babies, while the poor could not afford to invest even in a single wise one, all the while hiding from his flock his strong belief that their mindless procreation was in itself stupid, and had led to their destruction, and thus, craftily managed to build bases of angry and oppressed people wherever he walked. Walker had become a sophisticated thug. His lost love was driving him crazy, and though he realized that evil had sprouted within him, he watered it with Johnny, rationalizing his actions by reasoning that since it was the forbidden fruit of love that had made Adam and Eve aware of good and evil, with his love lost, evil was as good as good.

Walker was walking a straight and true path towards becoming a dictator. Walker's life had been filled with pain since childhood in spite of Walker laughing it all away every moment. He was, therefore, mad for nothing and about everything. If such a person can't become a great tyrant, nobody else can. The secret to Walker's supreme self-belief was that even though he had once been addicted to God, he was now free of the ordinary man's greatest addiction, making him God Himself, and since there was no more the fear of anything, including pain and death, he was also the Devil Himself. It was not known to anyone as to which religion, or religions, Walker's parents belonged to, for the irascible, abstruse, and arcane fellow never celebrated any festival, but instead, celebrated each and every day as a celebration of life. He did not believe in either right or wrong, but only in evolution whose sole aim was procreation; however, the madman did not believe in procreating himself, but only in sex as a means and an end in itself to enjoy life fueled by his Johnny. As for death, Walker walked hand in hand with it, for even though he was sick, he took no medication and rarely slept. These were the reasons for his insanity, and it is the stuff out of which great dictators are made.

Nobody had known Walker's true agenda initially. But the poor, the weak, and the wretched with whom he spent hours discussing, counselling, sharing, sympathizing, and empathizing slowly started to form an army behind him. They knew all the shortcuts in all domains, for a master is but a servant as he is dependent, and Walker began to use his comrades to weaken the non-communist infrastructure so that he and his army could demolish the unequal towers of money and build a monument of equality for humanity. This was Walker's agenda, and the reason why he walked in pain. Walker's creative communism was his own. He believed that people needed to be controlled thoroughly, not by men, but by laws. This germ had originated in Walker's brain, which had been out of his control, when it had decimated him. He had lost control because of a disgusting disease in his brain, and had been controlled by authoritarian doctors and other medical staff, following laws, who had tied him to a bed for months and medicated him into being a super-strong being, after which he had been finally discharged and let go of to roam free in the outside world. This germ had grown in power when he had realized that the Butterfly Effect of Physics proved that everything is affected by anything, and that each and every man destroys all others if not controlled. Walker was absolutely sure that men had to be controlled for their own benefit, or else they would annihilate themselves. He had also realized that man is nothing but his fertilization and environment, and thus, his firm belief in creative eugenics and creative communism came to be solidified and strengthened. Walker would be a dictator, for he knew that too many cooks spoil the broth, and also, that the disaster wrought by one man could be eliminated after eliminating just that one man, and by thus thinking, he became happy that there was an escape clause for humanity from all the sins he would in all probability commit upon it.

Walker would use the world's latest information technology to have spies who spied upon spies who spied upon spies, and so on and on, in a deadly web. In this manner, all would be reporting truthfully and completely on everybody, for they would be knowing that anything and everything they reported, or did not, could be easily verified by anybody, and that, if they lied, they would be executed. This procedure would eliminate the arrogance of the rich and the powerful and the meekness of the poor, the weak, and the wretched, all who would soon become equal. There would be no room for mischief either by the stupid or the dangerous, and the world would soon become a happy place. However, Walker planned to ban all media from carrying any kind of political news, for he knew that nothing good could be expected to come out from the commoner utilizing his precious time for the derailment of the state instead of for its betterment. Walker didn't understand the need for guns, missiles, fighter aircrafts, warships, and the such. His aim was to rid the world, one day soon, of such great inventions of human folly, though he knew perfectly well that when there were no more weapons left, men would beat and kick one another to death with their bare fists and naked feet until none were left; however, Walker wanted to delay the inevitable as long as possible, and hence his walk for the equality of humanity.

However, Walker would make it clear that equality would not mean sameness in society; uniqueness would be preserved for diversity and creativity. One of Walker's famous catchphrases for a creative communism was, "Which water should flow where should flow there", and therefore, he would give everybody the freedom to choose their own paths to success, and succeed his comrades would, for success, which is the offspring of true creativity – true creativity, which is the only true goal of all, or should be if it is not – is born only in the home of freedom. Walker's other equally popular catchphrases were, "Only in true creativity lies true liberty", "True freedom is the freedom to choose your work and work in freedom", "Wrong freedom is the freedom to have more wealth than others", "Freedom to work in liberty eradicates poverty". These catchphrases were symbolic of the creative communism innovated by Walker during his walks, and his army grew more and more day by day.

"Think for a moment, 'Why am I doing this?' or infinitely better yet, 'Why am I not doing that?' What stops you from being truly happy? Realize and then overcome the ignorance, false beliefs, untruths, conventions, conformations, servility, fears, and lack of a free enterprising spirit that stop you from living *your* life in absolute freedom…" This was part of a talk that Walker gave to the oppressed among whom there were a growing number of LGBTs.

Walker had wondered, *How to make the society move ahead?* and had come up with, *The poor, the weak, and the wretched, can only improve through creativity. They will find different passions other than mindlessly procreating. Creativity builds out of freedom of choice, and this freedom comes only when one is financially secure. Creative communism is the answer which will level the playing field. With equal opportunities for all, fueled by freedom of choice and then creativity, the overall economic and intellectual situation will improve dramatically and progress rapidly. No more will there be sweaty starved women labourers in tatters begging for a pittance from their masters which is absurdly less than their absolute right. Everyone must be taught how to develop a directing rational mind free from all negative emotions and feelings. With this concrete foundation laid, an empire of creative and economic riches can be built.*

Walker had also wondered, *Why creative eugenics?* He had seen the poor being born, suffer, and die poor and traumatized. He had seen many hospitals and doctors refusing to help without cash being paid upfront, and the sick poor living and dying in pain. Walker had realized that this suffering was unnecessary, and that the most stupid thing anyone could do in the world was to mindlessly procreate and bring more sufferers into this hell on earth when there was neither a God nor an economic means to justify the bringing of consciousnesses, whose default was suffering, into this world of suffering. *Only those who could alleviate their suffering with the help of pleasure, brought about by good genes and wealth, should be allowed to enter this world for the progress of the human race*, was what Walker's creative eugenics all about.

Walker had written in his diary, a diary which he kept so that he could understand himself, his drive, and purpose, more clearly, 'The poor are grateful and love you for one day after you indulge them with free money, and then, they start to hate you and eye hungrily the money you spend. The initially grateful become the sullen ungrateful. Their hate increases day by day. It is absolutely not their fault, and everybody knows why, and for those who deliberately fail to understand, I tell them, try having a simple meal with the innumerable starved right in front of you, eyeing you. I have understood this phenomenon over decades. Your well-to-do family, friends, acquaintances, and professional contacts advise you not to make friends with the so-called, "Lower Class", and not to spend your money upon them; however, it is actually the 'Lower Economic Class', and not, "Lower Class", for it is only money that takes one to good education, refined behaviour, acquired by exposure to the sublime things of the world, and more money, wealth, which the so-called "Upper Class" has in excess, and whose rightful money do the upper classes unrightfully have anyway, it is the lower classes'. The problem with the majority of the poor and a minority of the rich is mindless procreation, hoping that at least one of their progenies will make it bigger than themselves, and this is a perfect recipe for disaster, for resources are dissipated over the many children, and hence wasted, for none of them will have enough to truly succeed, whereas, if there had been only one child, it would have got more and adequate resources, enabling it to fire successfully. Animals are far better than humans, for only the strong mate, the weak die early, and there is no disease either of the mind or body. We human beasts need to learn from animals. The problem with life, and the reason for flags and armies, is that people are different in varied aspects, and mindless procreation, with limited resources on earth, makes for a disgruntled world, where one is ready to kill another for the basic necessities of life. People of one common denominator amalgamate to fight others with different common denominators, and soon, they themselves slowly disintegrate within an ingroup, finding different common denominators, leading to more fighting, and this war leaves all men alone in their unnecessary fight against an inevitable death. Men are inherently evil, and should be controlled by the less evil, who are so because of their better fertilization and environment.'

Walker used to say about his Johnny, which he imbibed religiously, hating the term, 'religion', that, "I don't enjoy it, but use it. Poison has to be imbibed to annihilate the poison in society." He also termed this his epiphany, hating the term 'epiphany', too. Walker was completely free of others and their weaknesses, and he had set forth with a vicious agenda of his own which would help others and kill him.

Walker had learnt something very, very profound. Until that moment of supreme learning, he had tried to be good to all people of all walks of life in all manner of ways. He had then foolishly built his future empire upon those few upon whom he had bestowed his unconditional love and lavish favours; however, when they had all begun cutting him off in an avalanche of their own disaster, Walker had had an "Epiphany". As a result, he immediately shrugged off all the Brutuses and began to live life in the moment, enjoying each and every new experience with someone new, and his future empire now came to be built upon not a permanent, but a transient foundation. The best part of it was that he no longer had to bear old friends, acquaintances, and relatives, most of who had turned traitors, and who with their goldfish memories, never had anything new to say, and the new ones who would certainly do the same after some time. Walker had realized that the universe was too big a place to bestow upon only a few his love and charity, when instead, he could expand into it with newer and newer people who, along with him, would realize a unified dream of equality through creativity.

After the Fishing Boat

After landing from the fishing boat, Walker was tired. No more was walking sane, one cannot walk on water, for one is not God. No One IS, so also, Walker, and he had used a boat; henceforth, Walker decided that he would also use vehicles to walk on land. It would be quicker, smoother, and more effective. Finally, the stupid stubborn Walker had given up his adamancy to stick to the asinine, which he loathed. Walker was, indeed, paradoxical.

Walker rode, walked, talked, roared, and rocked with the poor Caesars who quickly turned into Brutuses.

This made him question himself:

What is my mission?

Is my conscious vision the same as the purpose in my unconscious unconscious?

For Walker had realized that there was more to him than he himself knew.

By this time, Walker's technological spy-web was complete, giving news to the spider that there would be no more flies getting stuck in his web.

Later, Commie, the true revolutionary firebrand killed himself, after he tried to betray Walker, by sticking to one of Walker's agendas, but was instead betrayed by Walker who loved none who tried to stick to him or his ideas, limiting his freedom.

The last conversation between Commie and Walker:

Commie: "Do not retaliate, but quietly understand the enemy, your loved ones, and when the time comes for the push to be transformed into a shove, really retaliate, crushing all, for if you can crush your loved ones, you can crush anybody else.

"It is all about being a pearl-atom-bomb in your secret-oyster-bunker that annihilates the fist that tries to destroy its freedom.

"Men are led by asinine prophets towards stupid destruction, and you, Walker, were the best and worst of them all.

"Walker, your words were the bullets in the guns that disgruntled men and women bought for themselves to escape their wretchedness, and thus, your war was funded by your soldiers themselves, proving that you, Walker, were the shrewdest of prophets.

"You did not have a family which could be targeted in lieu of you, for you had distanced yourself from, no, to be precise, cut off your entire immediate and extended family from yourself.

"Today, you have no one when things have escalated to a phase where there are no winners, but only losers, Hyenas."

Walker: "If one feels powerful because of other powerful people, one is actually powerless."

Commie: "Vultures are men who refuse to acknowledge, young fools, lest they grow into rebels, and not Cows after understanding the Vultures and their Hyenas."

Flower, and a much older than Walker, his alter ego, Thinker, eloped from the spider's web, mad about the maddening maddened Walker.

The last conversation between Flower and Walker:

Flower: "What is the Soul, Walker?"

Walker: "Simple babe, it is the you in you, the 'I', the inner inner that dictates the outer from the outer."

Flower: "What!"

Walker: "The chemical conscience which has been transferred through your ancestors' genes, helping them to survive and multiply, babe!"

The last conversation between Thinker and Walker:

Walker: "I want to be ordinary!"

Thinker: "No, you can't be. You have already damned yourself to extraordinariness. Only those proud of their body, bodies in whatever conditions, can walk proudly nude on nude beaches, so also those who are proud of their minds, for very good reasons, can let them wander anywhere in all their nakedness, hiding nothing. Everyone is scared of the naked Walker, one who has neither anything to hide nor lose.

"How many ideas have to die before your idea is the only one left surviving?"

Walker: "Truth and justice, and the outcome of laws acted upon, both need not be the same.

"No good thing presents itself to anyone. Good things have to be strived for, and even if not even one of them comes to one, one while striving for the good will have at the least lived a good life in the positive."

Thinker: "You are a masochist, Walker."

Walker: "I am proudly proud of being a masochist, for it was those whom I lovingly loved who had been doing the tortuous torturous torturing. Nobody can call me ungrateful!

"I am not a bad man, but unfortunately, for both myself and others, I need to and become bad when faced with bad; my bad opposing my good, expressing the embracing conflict of my Yin and Yang inherent to the whole world, against and for which I am fighting for, and this is the saga of Walker, a walker who tried to walk against life all the while knowing that there was no way in which he could win, or lose.

"One can't be strong outside without strength inside, and the only way to build up an invincible arsenal inside is to work the inside into a state which will devastate both the inside and the outside; absolute freedom through work."

The thought of Flower and Thinker before they eloped together:

A time will come, definitely for all of us, when we have to move away from all that we love and all those who love us, in order to be truly loved by ourselves, for we are the only ones who truly love ourselves, and if we do not distance ourselves from love, we will never ever realize what love truly is.

Soldier and Adder got married, but stayed with Walker.

It is but only the nearest and dearest to one that betray one, and Walker was those betrayers, betraying himself.

Walker finally crumbled, courtesy of his frail legs of both body and mind.

Very few, of the innumerable who had followed Walker in his once gigantic army, now walked with him, for he had become too complex even for himself.

To rise into catching a shark, the fisherman must release those small fish who have taken the bait meant for a great enemy. If we stay amongst the small, trying to prove we are great, we will become small with the anchors of smallness dragging us down. When our bait fails, we must sink down to where the sharks are, to rise higher than we have ever been.

None saw a good future with Walker, or for Walker, but those who loved him, stuck unconditionally with him.

Even those who stuck to him thought, *Walker is insane. He can't control either his mind or body, so wants to control others!*

While Walker thought simultaneously, *I will do my best, my duty, and let them all go to hell later!*

PART 2
SELENE

Walker's Last Hurrah

Walker walked with his less than plentiful, many a dirty dozen.

He tried to explain to Adder, "My *Creative Communism* was about a tilting balance which would have left the mental winning. All the needs of all would have been satisfied, but mental ability would have determined who would be shunted to the back of the physical, and since nobody likes that, the physical would have strived to be the mental, and eventually, machines would have relieved all of all.

Walker had been, and was, too complex for Adder, her husband Soldier, and everyone else.

For Walker, the sun never heralded the day, but the moon, the full, the new, and all its phases in-between did. For him, change, and only change, held any real value. Under the light and darkness, and also a varying mixture of both, he felt a true bliss in which nothing was amiss.

It was an inkling of what would come, very soon, as he thought about his thoughts with Johnny the Scot, who was a true samurai blade compared to the whiskey-axes of barbarians.

Walker had become a powerful walker simply because he was innocent; innocent, that is, to his conscious mind, and that was what people had seen Walker as. The stains that had tainted his pristine white had come to be looked upon as blasphemous battle wounds inflicted upon a walking God; wounds, which were still to Walker, of immense revolutionary significance and hence, value, which fortunately or unfortunately, were all the time injecting their poison into him; however, almost all the people of Walker had wised up to the true Walker leaving him poisoned by himself.

Walker's thoughts screamed to Walker:

If you could be, you would not be, and in the end, I am only I, nothing more, nothing less!

More over few, it is always wanting to be the majority, to enslave the minority!

Which honest man doesn't deserve respect, or for that matter, any man, for I strongly believe no mother gives birth to a completely dishonest child!

We are all on our way to becoming old, but wise? It all depends on how much we can endure and forgive, most importantly, ourselves, realizing we are all but only human and near our ends. If we can fall in love, with primarily ourselves, and then with one another, knowing truly well that there is no supernatural other but only the universal our, we will all be eternally blissful together.

Selene

As Walker was on his last legs during the last legs of his walk, he found himself unable to love himself or the journey he had embarked upon anymore. His walk slowed down as no more was the dangerous fool galloping towards death brandishing his two swords, one of which, the double-edged sword, had slashed him more than others' ideas, innumerable others' ideas which he had branded his enemies, when the actual harsh truth that he had failed miserably to realize was that others and their ideas were one and the same entities. Therefore, now the ghastly mental intellectual wounds he had inflicted upon others that were obviously physical, for the mental is the physical, had as their twins his own wounds. His body and mind, which had been battered long before he had started on his walk, were now on their last legs. One blazing afternoon when Walker and his tiny band of die-hard loyalists sat dispersed under the feeble shades of a few withered leaves of sparse sparse trees, not at all trying to move even a little and breathe in the burning breeze and unable to look at one another in the eyes as a result of their self-inflicted wounds, the morose Walker, through his dying eyes, spied an elegant lady of dignified bearing who was walking all alone on the burning asphalt with her head held high, oblivious to the scalding asphalt below and the savage sun above, treading her own middle path with sublime grace and cooling the fiercely hot breeze with the cool breaths of her mind.

Walker's heart, which he had been oblivious of until now, much like innumerable other truly good and default gifts of life, started pounding and caused his withered lips to mouth a mournful plea, *Help…* a silent plea which transcended the ugly fort Walker had built around himself and reached the free spirit who was spiritedly on her way with true spirituality in search of the ultimate spiritual experience. It is only such people who hear and respond to the weak, the poor, and the wretched with kindness, empathy, and sympathy, and the walker woman's ears, which were her heart, upon hearing the plea of the broken walker, Walker, made her stop her walk in the direction she was headed and divert the direction of her walk towards Walker who was no more walking, but dying. As she stood over the sitting Walker, with his back resting against a gnarled tree trunk, blocking the angry sun with her fragile head, her lips curved and gently smiled. This was the water, the stuff of life, the parched Walker had been searching for all his life. But Walker still had a lot of Walker left in him. He imposed himself on his benefactor by saying the first words that came into his mind, and not those which were in his heart, "I need soldiers for my cause. You will fit in as you too are a walker like me." To which the lady said nothing, but simply sat down with the men of war until all were ready to walk again in the cool night. It was a full moon night and as Walker walked ahead of his tribe, the woman simply chose to follow behind everyone else, which Walker noticed. Feeling a supreme feeling of triumph over the helpless *Help…* he had mouthed in the direction of the spirited walker's walking, Walker felt that he could now safely descend from his throne and fall back to converse and convert the beautiful woman, who he insanely thought was following him, with his ideas. After a few hours of preaching to her under the jaundiced full moon, he again insanely thinking that he had conquered her, her mind, because of the silence enveloping her, said haughtily, "It is the rightful duty of a leader to give a name to his new follower, and therefore, on this moonlit night, I dub thee, Selene," and immediately vanished ahead into his dark night in spite of the all-enveloping gentle glow of the moon. The silence enveloping the now Selene had not been a flimsy garment to hide shame, but a cloak of armour against all the insane ideas of the world, and soon, she would not walk behind Walker, but with Walker behind her, for it is only a leader who is first a follower, in order to understand, even, and foremost, the enemy, and then transcend in her own individuality.

Walker's Emotional Reasoning Muse

It was a dreary evening, wet and cold, with the cowardly sun weeping copiously behind overlapping dark blankets over which brilliant white fireflies were streaking at the speed of light, and predatory birds were zigzagging inside the black blankets screeching thunderously and trying to make a prey of the fireflies. But light is faster than sound, not simply the light of reason, but the light of reason in whose veins flows the blood of emotion, and this light blinds the sounds of words, which, consciously or unconsciously, are incessantly striving to convert other sounds to their own frequency to attain a destructive resonance. Destructive resonance, because in universal sameness without individuality lie the graves of great creative ideas. In nature, no vigorous predator becomes its prey's prey. But in the world of men, each one is another's predator and prey, and the worst predators are the men of sound, the rhetorical orators, sad old men, sad and old in either mind or body or both, who wish to become happy by snatching away the happiness of others to fill their empty hearts, and therefore instigate hate and violence among the myriad unhappy others. Others who are too ignorant to realize that they are but cannon fodder, and become false martyrs in a war which nobody wins. But since men are one another's predator and prey, a fact which had become crystal clear to Walker the moment he had started observing and thinking at a very early age, he had reasoned unemotionally that the only way to achieve world peace and equality was if the downtrodden prey turned predator under the leadership of a wise philosopher, like himself. However, a disturbingly disturbing fact, which he had lied about to, and deceived with a dark deception, himself, was that in reality, men are not equal simply because of each man's unique fertilization and environment, and he had blindly started upon his goal to communize, even though creatively, the world, even though in his unconscious unconscious, he had known an insane solution, the *Tower to God*, which proposed capitalism and communism in alternate steps incorporating eugenics for a better world in which he would be the last free man standing on earth, a God.

After Walker had fooled both himself and the intelligent unwise men whose minds he had conquered as to the real purpose behind his desire to invest his personal machine with emotion – a machine which would one day escalate into a universal machine courtesy of Walker's unconscious unconscious, a supposedly moral conscious machine without emotion which would supposedly rule over a world unified by him after he supposedly abdicated and relinquished all his powers to it – he had happily set about coding illogic into a logical program, trying to make possible the impossible, to incorporate illogical emotion, which incorporates within itself insane conflict, into his budding logical personal machine, drawing from the illogic of the only intelligent animal in nature, man, being both his own predator and prey, and succeeded.

After Walker had finished relating the story of his unbelievable yet actualized victory of incorporating illogic within logic to Selene in a tiny cave where both they and his men were taking shelter from the angry elements outside, she quietly posed a question to him while staring deep into the volatile drama in the sky, "So, since you are capable of emotional reasoning, why are your hard-headed philosophies based upon harsh rationalism?" Walker, who, too, was staring into the same direction as she, laughed and replied trying to make out what volatile drama was being inspired in her mind by the one in the sky, "But that was only coding, not an irrational life which needs to be set rational by me!" Selene smiled. Closing her eyes as if all things volatile, both inside and outside, had ceased said peacefully, "Love is irrational, but that is precisely what the whole world desperately needs right now. I am sure you can code it into humanity..."

Selene's Equality

Walker's tiny, dirty army, soggy with the sweat of exhaustion, reached a quaint ramshackle inn just as the smiling sun rose in all its splendour, refreshed after moonlighting in a better part of the world, but which immediately frowned and blazed again beholding a decaying town in a sadder part of the world, and Walker's men, who had not encountered a watering hole for days, were delighted at the prospect of having a good time, and finally relaxed after being under a constantly increasing volcanic pressure by their mercurial leader to change the world for the better in the manner which he had thought best, always.

Upon entering and washing off the grime on their faces and arms as best as they could with the little dirty water that was available for that purpose, aided by their generous sweat which was saltier but cleaner, the army of walkers commandeered most of the unoccupied tables and chairs after disposing off the previous day's physical memories of others. All, except Walker and Selene, ordered the cheap drinks which they had become accustomed to as a result of their incessant walking only through poor areas.

Walker reached into his backpack and brought out his constant walking companion, his Johnny, and after offering to pour a drink for Selene – Selene who was sitting relaxedly beside him on one of the inn's coarse wooden chairs, smiling at the charm that had suddenly replaced the weariness on Walker's face that had begun to glow more and more as he held and beheld the glass garment of his lover, who would soon in small quantities seductively slip out of her seductive green transparent clothes, and seduce her lover with her intoxication – an offer that was waved away by a dainty hand with a dainty flip of it, started warming himself up with his lover.

After a red flush began permeating Walker's face, Selene laughingly told her leader, "You are in love," to which, Walker replied melancholically, "Yes, immoral ladies are more moral than moral ones who think they have the moral right to judge your morality and find it in their morals to stab you in the back after you have sacrificed your morality to defend their morals. Nobody and nothing should be indispensable in life. Not even life itself. The only thing that should be held onto with love and passion for forever is one's purpose after distilling the entire world with all its conflicting ideologies with a directing rational mind, to formulate a unique ideology for oneself that gives one one's true and invincible purpose in life. No weak woman, or for that matter no weak man, cannot and should not be a permanent fixture of a strong man's life, for the dissatisfaction in the weak brought about by boredom, a result of them lacking a strong purpose in life, and greed, again in the weak, brought about by their blindness to existing unopened gifts and a constant hankering for more, more of what which is not at all clear to them or will ever be, both aid them, the weak, in coming up with ingenious potent moral poisons to lace the elixir of the strong."

Selene was shocked, "What you must have gone through to become what you are now, you poor, poor soul!" Pretty Selene and

Walker's ugly words had drawn all the unemployed locals, who had graced the inn earlier in the morning than Walker's company, around their table. As all the haggard men and women stood in a circle, looking on at the two strong ones with bewildered awe, and also pitifully scrutinizing Walker's enchantingly exotic lover and her garment, Walker the man, and not Walker the leader, rose to the occasion, and quickly getting up from his coarse wooden throne, himself set about bringing empty chairs to his and Selene's table, and asking the incredulous locals to join them, which they gracefully did, he unselfishly shared his lover with his new friends until there was not even a drop left of her.

Immediately after the costly bottle became just another cheap empty bottle, the cheap friends vanished even faster than they had come, at which, Walker, the leader, started laughing merrily, and leaning confidentially towards Selene, who was the only other now left at their table, said in a whisper, "My dream of equality needs me to rule these men into rising and becoming my equals," to which, she sadly replied, leaning away from his breath, "Walker, I have studied and understood you, your vision, mission, and methods. I agree with your unconscious unconscious that nobody is equal to another, and a euphemism for sad inequality would be that some are more equal than others, but ruling is not the answer, for even the best rulers in history to date have miserably failed to bring about true equality," at which, Walker, whose mouth was now maintaining a certain distance from Selene's nose, whose entire span his breath would not be able to travel, said proudly, "You have done your homework on me, good! I won't ask why, because I am the man most in the news for long, and everybody, both my friends and my enemies, who either love me or hate me, or both, are terribly curious about what makes Walker, Walker, and mark, there is only one ingroup and one outgroup with respect to me, one is either for me or against me, for I do not believe in grey areas," and then haughtily, "and pray, what is *your* solution to transform inequality into equality?" Selene leaned forward this time, and as Walker maintained his position, replied calmly, "There is a simple method. Treat everybody as your equal, even though knowing the truth that no one ever truly is, and teach this to your children and others' children too. In time, with the process repeating, the world will achieve equality without the loss of anyone's individuality. Just a little while ago, I saw you implementing my simple method with the greatest simplicity I have ever observed in any man, so tell me, Walker, why do you run from Walker?"

Selene's Creativity

Suddenly, in the early evening, Walker's scalded unit that had been caught in a maze of dry rocky hills playing fiercely intense rallies incessantly since dawn with burning balls of the blazing sun, succeeded in getting through the heat-trap. They were staggered to see an antithesis of the torture chamber they had been released from, for what was inviting the grievously wounded soldiers into its healing embrace was a soft green lush uneven bed decked here and there with delicate flowers, of myriad hues, fanned by gentle air currents from different directions capturing the various aromas of diverse flowers and mingling at manifold junctions to allow their innovative amalgamated perfumes to disembark in the cool refreshing ambience. Walker's men became boys and ran yelling exuberantly with arms raised high in great gratitude into the paradise, all in different directions in search of their own piece of a vibrant peace, while Selene and Walker, watching them like indulgent doting parents, followed their children slowly taking delicate sips of the nectar before them. They soon found a placid pool to sit beside and quench their thirst for the true meaning of creativity. Walker ran, "It is in solitude that creativity grows in leaps and bounds…" after which, Selene walked softly, "Agreed, but having read your criminal record that details your multitudinous arrests by the creativity police for having perpetrated atrocious crimes upon your own creativity innumerable times, I wish to say that, *solitude does not mean loneliness*. What you once had considered to be your supreme solitude was actually, in harsh reality, your sad loneliness, and a lonely creativity is a destructive creativity. There is only so much that one can find within without going without. The redundant polishing of the blade of such a lonely creativity sword causes it to vanish and be replaced by a dangerous imaginary creativity sword which is distorted in such a hideous manner that it can be used only for hideous purposes, to destroy. Such a sword destroys one's within first before emerging bloodied and bloodthirsty for the without, while a true creativity sword only annihilates the sickness of ordinariness and brings in the reign of wonder, who is the mother of evolved creativities." Then, falling silent, Selene gracefully extended her arm with its hand cupped. Within seconds, a tiny butterfly, whose vibrant colours could challenge any rainbow, came flitting delicately and alighted in her cup seeking the nectar of creativity. Walker, who was absorbing all like a white sponge, dunked in red wine, suddenly exclaimed, "Creativity descends upon one when one is not clutching, but releasing…"

Walker's Suicide

It was a cool soft cloudy dawn with even the high-spirited birds, usually yelling in the early morning at lazy worms, to quickly wake up and pop their heads out of the earth to have a look at the fresh beauty of a brand new day outside so that they could pop them on their noggins and increase the beauty of their morning by having the breakfast of kings, toning down their exuberance and whispering gently to the worms to come join them for breakfast, played their part in singing the song of a calm morning. But it was the calm before a storm; a storm, which would kill Walker's desire for immortality. Walker and Selene were walking that gentle morning in fields of green. Tall and slender lush green grass shot up in every direction like mother nature's hair standing on end and gently swaying in the cool fragrant zephyr. She shook her head in shock with a premonition of what Walker was planning to do. Walker, with his hands clasped behind his back and eyes staring deep into the earth, which his boots were heavily treading, broke the silence of that peaceful morning by broaching to Selene in calm even tones, "My personal mind machine is ready and fully capable of sustaining my mind for eternity. However, I have decided not to allow it to escalate into a universal machine, as was my hidden dark desire inside my falsified desires, my black wish that you helped me unearth and bring out into the light with your gift to me of emotional reasoning, for me to smite down for the benefit of all. But I am going to plug myself into it and upload my mind, immediately, for I am sure the broken twin wings of my body and mind will soon be incapable of flight. Before I hit the ground and my body is consumed by earth, my mind has to be set free from the shackles of its body to transcend into infinity and eternity."

A single bird, detached from its flock as a result of an insane hunger which had kept it digging for more and more worms in the dirt, instead of being satisfied with what had already been generously gifted to it by mother nature, was now screeching and flying around in circles searching for its flock which would have no more truck with the bird whose mind was stuck in muck. Looking up at the devastated lonely bird above their heads for a full silent minute, and then, sideways at Walker, Selene spoke, "Any want almost always leads to wanting more. Since it is neither a need nor a necessity, but usually an invalid desire, it often leads to trouble. And here we are not simply talking about simple trouble, but a bottomless quagmire into which you desperately want to jump with scuba gear enhanced with an infinite supply of breathable air. Trust me, it is not at all going to be even in the least bit pleasant even before a short period of time has elapsed, for you will be alone," and looking back up again at the bird, which was still lost, she continued, "for eternity. It will not be your consciousness which will torture you forever, but your emotions which will kill and yet keep you alive – every moment – in excruciating agony for eternity. It is a fate worse than death." Walker suddenly heard the crying bird, which had been crying incessantly and copiously for a long time. Turning his face upwards towards its agonized flapping for the first time, he slowly spoke, "There is room for one more in my machine. I can upload your emotions along with your consciousness and allow them to run on the emotional software I had developed for myself…" Selene was softly firm, "The fact of life is death, and I would like to live that life, however short or painful it is, for that is the only way one can ever truly live fully." The bird above suddenly realized that it was flying around in circles, and that if it continued along the same path, it would soon drop dead without getting anywhere. Therefore, it went off at a tangent hoping that it had found a beneficial direction. The storm had killed Walker's desire for immortality, and he gave the order for his suicide, immediately after which, his soldiers began the journey to the nearest and fiercest volcano to feed Walker's machine into the inferno-smitten belly of a beast from hell.

The idea of the personal turning universal machine had failed, simply because the men, including first and foremost Walker himself, to be connected and transferred to the machine, had failed. Such connections could not have been allowed to survive for eternity, over infinity. Hence, space and time, the coupled Gods, had freed themselves from Walker and his humanity.

Walker's Enlightenment

It was a full moon night like the one on which Walker had dubbed Selene, Selene, but the moon was not jaundiced like it had been on that night, instead, it was a clear glowing pearl-white, and both the follower and the leader were sitting on the banks of a pristine lake which glowed ethereally, drowning out the distant stars the follower, once leader, had insanely strived for, and enlightened him slowly but truly and completely for the first time, and the once madman realized that he was the luckiest man to have ever walked the earth, for the moon had always been with him, supporting, guiding, and encouraging him to shrug off all, even himself, and look without, and not within, at the beauty which was within the reach of each and every man, but which most, most infamously himself, as he had once shunned, shun with a callous and cynical attitude the greatest gift one can be gifted, life itself. True enlightenment requires confession, and then acceptance, not by the person being confessed to, but by the confessor himself, of himself. The Walker of the moment was poised to leap over the canyon overflowing with his past insanity to land on the pinnacle of a sane enlightenment, where a pure white light shone, beckoning him like nothing else had ever done before as he confessed to Selene, "I had always known that Shoonya, nothing and everything, was birth and death, before and after which there was and will be nothingness. Only this half-knowledge, the most dangerous kind of knowledge, had me galloping insanely and fearlessly from nothing towards nothing, disregarding the splendid spectrum of life in-between. As a result, all I ever gained, was nothing; agreed that a certain something, my creativity, existed, but with a heart, added to my mind, I could have accomplished anything, that anything being a supreme creativity which is everything; a creativity which does not shine for the creator alone, causing him to shine alone in darkness, but a constructive creativity amidst humanity which shines for all to dispel the darkness from wretched minds and hearts. You made me realize this, Selene, and maybe it is too late for me to embrace this supreme creativity, but you, you already have; however, creation is self-actualization, a never-ending process, a process whose Yang grows stronger with an increasing understanding of Yin, the dark, which is the curse of humanity. Now since you have befriended and understood the most infamous warrior-slave of Yin, I am sure your creativity will keep on transcending all the collective barriers which imprison men within the cold dark dungeons of their minds and set them free as you have set me free." Selene smiled in acceptance, and Walker found himself on the pinnacle of enlightenment looking up serenely into the night-sky at the moon.

Finis

The Hyenas were replaced by Walker's men, the new Hyenas of his making, but the new ones were weak, selfish, and overflowing with hypocrisy, for they had never ever been true soldiers before they became Hyenas, but only slaves, and then, these new Hyenas started killing off one another to gain control of the Cows, with packs disintegrating into degenerate loners, leading to the killing of Cows decreasing drastically, for lack of organization. New Cows, not understanding creative eugenics, began procreating mindlessly and formedthe third wave of Hyenas, while Vultures, having no sufficient carrion to eat, started dying out quickly, which after a stage led to decaying flesh contaminating the ecosystem. With no more Lions left, the ones surviving the old Hyenas, having been polished off by the new loner Hyenas, having become too weak to even survive a single Hyena with its jaws able to crunch their brittle old brave bones into smithereens, there were no more ideal idealistic leaders left, but only rabble in the rubble. The war had been for nothing, but everything had regressed to square minus one. Walker's mind, which had never ever taken even a single short break, in his entire life, had finally ground to a halt. Having been soothed by Selene, Walker, once more, had become a writer and a poet in order to document a sad epic saga so that it would never ever be repeated again, but…

Would Walker's insane volatile deformed creativity, contained, tempered, and shaped by calmly glowing Selene's, writing the sad saga, a saga led by him, be able to douse an infernal fate, almost reserved by themselves, by all those whom he had loved, hated, loved, and so on and on, and who would bequeath their misery to their progenies, their progenies to their progenies, and so on and on, and shape a warmly pleasant future for all, after another bone-marrow-chilling episode of cold-blooded humanity's attempted suicide with an ice-cold dagger – redundancy upon adjective overladen redundancy, killing the pure blood of creativity…

At the end of the day, what did Walker truly wish?

And what about Selene? Where was she? Probably transcending mortality to show misguided men like Walker the right walk to walk.

After Walker used to sit down skewedly with one of his part-alter egos, Thinker, thinking, he used to return to reality's Sufferer, and convulse with him in pain, like a true sufferer.

After Walker, with his Soldier, another one of his part-alter egos, having done his soldiering, having dismembered hapless hyenas and vintage vultures, he used to again merge with Sufferer, and insufferably suffer.

With Adder, another one of his part-alter egos, Walker used to become an adder, adding to both others' and his suffering and become an inseparable part of Sufferer, adding the solace of sex to suffering.

And even in Flower, Walker had seen Sufferer.

Commie was, but an anachronism.

The only truth of Walker's life was the suffering of Sufferer, Sufferer, who the real Walker was.

Epilogue

Walker had realized that neither he nor anyone could reform the world. That it would have to reform itself. Each and every man himself until the whole started becoming better and better exponentially with time, a positively inclined juggernaut over all of space. He had accepted the fact that the God fallacy would stay and have to stay until each and every man became enlightened, accepted his mortality, and no more being scared of death, still was not galloping towards it with an iron fist crushing the skulls of others for his own pleasure sure that there was no supernatural karma, but only the karma between living beings, which he knew most escaped. Walker was also convinced of something incredible - that the really enlightened figures in history actually knew the truth about the God fallacy, but had brought in God, religion, and their associated philosophies to tame the brutish man, to empower the poor, weak, and wretched man so that true evolution could take place while keeping their enlightenment about this enlightened knowledge a secret. Maybe, actually, in all probability, something had really gone wrong with this method, but it was the only way, the path of least resistance towards a better human until someday, somebody could find a better way. But it would not be Walker. Walker had stopped walking and again started writing. This was his only contribution to true human evolution.

THE DARK

Setting One's Life on Fire to Make One's Words Shine Brighter

The Dark

It was the dark amidst neon lights clamouring for customers.

It was the dark amidst stadium lights clamouring for fans.

It was the dark amidst the backlit smartphones, tablets, and laptop screens clamouring for young minds.

It was the dark for books.

It was the 'Dark Ages' for books.

The descendants, of ancestors who had wolfed down books by candlelight like werewolves on a rampage, were complacent with being fed electronic mind-junk by both political and non-political actors intent upon the rampant spreading of their money-making propagandas.

The Old Writer and The Young Boy

But, as always, there were a few dissenters.

One was the old writer who refused to give up writing in spite of penury and another was a little boy mesmerised by old books so much that he used to smell each page's history before he read it.

The writer and the sniffer were one of a kind, because, without the reader, there is no writer. They complemented each other without having ever met.

The writer lived in a slum with the luxury of an old computer and a printer, while the little boy lived in a mansion which had been constructed on a piece of land which had been grabbed from the slum in which the writer lived.

Actually, they were neighbours.

What separates people is not land, but knowledge, and the writer and the reader were already chums through the printed word.

The writer had been writing for long and the boy had been but not for long born. The writer had never become either a husband or a father and the boy had an intellectual father like the writer who showered books upon him while not knowing that most of them had been written by the writer a portion of whose slum's land he had bought with the force of his money.

The writer, who had exhausted all the philosophy of the world, very early, and had become a children's book writer, had been thus introduced to his neighbour.

The writer was a coward when it came to concrete financial matters, and hence he was poor, but he was courageous when it came to the realms of the abstract mind, and hence he was rich when it came to life's spiritual matters.

He knew that spiritual need not mean supernatural, and was thus incredible and invincible.

But he was a criminal. He was committing a heinous crime upon children. He was writing books for them while hiding the truth he had realized from them.

He knew they were not his children and he had no right to impose his views upon them. Therefore, he lied to them without lying to them. He hid his views in arcane fables for the feeble of the mind.

But the young boy, his neighbour, was not to be fooled. He read, read, and reread his neighbour who he did not know was his neighbour and wished to meet the anonymous author who was trying to fool his young mind into believing something which the author did not.

Thus began a relationship which a mighty ship captained by the young boy set sail upon.

The writer lived in a shabby cabin with a torn roof which opened out into shiny stars at night, and that was when he wrote his twinkling fables for the young stars on Earth.

He wrote to tell them of immense possibilities yet hid from them tiny impossibilities like life after death and God.

He had to live with his curse of not being able to tell the truth of life and death to innocent younglings.

His most famous fable ran as follows:

The child looked at the sky and marvelled. Its parents told it that it was looking at God. The child, in all its innocence, asked back, "But isn't God looking back at me?" The happy parents answered, "Yes, dear!" Then the suddenly exuberant child exclaimed, "Life is a mirror!"

Nobody thankfully understood the fable and the writing fetched the writer many months respite from poverty.

The stupid writer had then tried to explore time in his next fable:

A donkey was trying to understand time. Its owner said that it was an ass for trying to do so. The smart-ass heehawed, "Isn't time birth and decay, birth and decay? If so, what really lives and dies in the multiverse? If so, doesn't time not exist, for the multiverse has always existed in one form or another?"

The exasperated owner beat his good donkey while shouting, "Do you measure everything by life, you ass!"

The poor enlightened donkey brayed, "Isn't this only life all we have to measure everything by?"

The owner sold the donkey to a sage with the thought that both would gel well.

The sage and the ass lived happily ever after while the previous owner was consumed by the time he hadn't an inkling of.

This fable put the writer into the legions of contemptible writers trying to understand the unknown.

Fortunately, the writer bore the hurt on his heart as a medal and continued writing for children even though he had yet not thrown off his dunce's cap of philosophy.

The problem with writing children's books with hidden meanings was that children, who had wonder written large upon their minds, hearts, and faces, had no money to buy the writer's books, which they certainly would have loved, while their parents who had purchasing power, were already deadened to the writer's marvels or else were deeply scared of the writer's books because of the truths hidden behind the writer's ambiguity which was beyond their comprehension. Thus, most parents who suffocated their kids with their love didn't buy the writer's books for their children, to keep them safe from truths they didn't understand, which kept on making the writer poorer and poorer the more and more he wrote.

The Search

But the young boy's rich father had given his very young son both intellectual and financial independence, and the young boy had taken to roaming the slum adjacent to his mansion.

He had loved the derelict shop which sold many second-hand books and also the writer's new books which had been foisted upon him by his publisher as a result of them not selling enough copies. The writer had to pay for his unsold books and try to sell them himself if he wanted to keep on being published. The writer had started young at writing, and growing older, had adopted a pen name 'Anon' to keep from being ridiculed by society for being a failure. Only the bookstall owner who sold second-hand books and the writer's new unsold books knew his identity as a writer, and kept it a closely guarded secret. All else thought of the writer as a derelict.

Now the young boy loved Anon and used to wait eagerly for every new book of Anon's to be added to the bookshelf of the derelict shop so that he could splurge his father's money on Anon and his quickly developing intellect.

The young boy's infatuation with Anon had been conveyed by the owner of the derelict bookshop to the writer, and the writer, whenever a new book of his was published, used to wait with grandfatherly love beside the shop for days until the young boy came kicking his heels in the air to buy a book from his beloved writer.

It is always the old who know the young and the young who fail to recognize the old.

So it was with the writer and his young fan.

But it is always the old who derive the greatest pleasure from such interactions.

The writer's pocket was a little full because of the young boy.

The writer's another, and only other luxury was an old fridge. He used to keep it stocked with cold water and used to keep on gulping incessantly from one cold water bottle after another from morning till night, to stave off hunger, and at night, when his stomach was too cramped to accept food, he used to eat the little he could afford to keep up the fight for life.

Meanwhile, the young boy used to drown in honey cakes while reading the latest from Anon till his stomach ached and mind grew numb.

The writer was naughty. When once he used to drink scotch when his insipid books sold like hot cakes, he now used to drink cheap whiskey after the frugal sales of his intellectual books.

But the kick now was higher and brighter, and the naughty boy enjoyed his punishment. The writer was masochistic, to say the least.

Masochism is wonderful when one is right.

The writer was happy with his small stuff as he knew he was dealing with the big stuff.

When one lights a small lamp in the dark for a poor kid to study, it is better than lighting a stadium for a fool to hit a ball into idiots worshipping him.

The writer loved his cheap booze and no food. The young boy loved his plush food and no booze. What a combination! Opposites are what love is made of.

They loved each other without having recognized each other completely.

Such a love is the most precious of all loves.

The writer used to dream. When young his dreams were full of vibrant hopes and he used to get up refreshed and raring to go in the morning. But as he got older and older, his dreams started decaying and so did his mornings. That's why he was a creature of the night who rarely slept, afraid of what dreams may come.

Dreams are but our worst fears and desires, and the writer's old love used to come and go in his dreams and this made him a madman unable to sleep and face his dreams.

But the young boy had made a difference in the old life of the writer. He had brought a grandchild into the life of a granddad who had never married or procreated.

Our own sons and daughters do not follow our philosophy which we have tried so hard to refine, but here was an unrelated kid who was madly searching for his educator who was neither his father nor grandfather.

Such relationships are the relationships of stars that the ordinary human who doesn't look up can never understand.

Men live in fear of the unexpected and children in anticipation of the unexpected. But the old writer was a young boy. After all, what is old but a state of the mind and not the state of the body? Looking inversely, the young boy was old. For after all wisdom is an old man's game but the young boy already had some of it.

The young boy's intuition made him roam the slum and haunt the derelict bookshop in his search for Anon. But the writer was a chameleon who hid himself from his searcher in inventive manners. For example, he used to appear as a beggar, which was not difficult given his conditions, in front of the bookshop and beg the boy for alms so that a poor old man can have a small drink. The young boy, who, like all fresh bodies, despised drinking, immediately wrote off the dirty drunk he regularly saw as being Anon. Thus, the old writer, who loved the young boy, and wished to remain anonymous, could enjoy his company without being recognized, albeit for only a few moments in which he was given the cold shoulder.

Love does not mean recognition. This the old writer knew, but the young boy did not, and hence he desperately tried to put a face to the writer he loved. But the writer cannot be said to have implemented this philosophy himself, for he haunted the outsides of the huge compounds of the young boy's mansion in desperate attempts to catch a glimpse of his innocent face behind high large windows reading, his or another's books. This was because the writer was a masochist and his brain refused to remember the innocent beauty of the young boy's face each and every time after he had seen him last.

It is difficult to say whether all this was the writer's love of writing or having his writing read, or simply a search for innocent love, an innocent love between a writer and a reader, or more deeply, an old man's search for progeny which he had failed to have.

Every man, no matter how strong, desires a woman's love and progeny no matter how ungrateful.

But here was the writer being again ungrateful to himself by first not having had his own family and now rejecting the young boy's love.

It was because all loves are not sublime, and many are more than dangerous.

The writer knew that to put an old mind into a young heart was nothing short of cutting short its lifespan.

Thus, he avoided recognition by the young boy like the plague.

Philosophy One

But he was a criminal nonetheless. It was because he still wrote children's books with the masked mind and heart of a philosopher.

There are three levels on the podium of life's sport. On the bronze level stands the confrontationist, on the silver level stands the non-confrontationist who values his own peace above all else, but the gold medallist is the non-confrontationist, who, though valuing his own peace more than platinum, confronts the confrontationist for the sake of peace for all, while during the whole while sacrificing his own peace, and wins the gold in the game of life.

There is no platinum medal in life's game. A peaceful death is the platinum medal.

And for the rest, those who stand in the grey area between winning and losing are but in Purgatory.

The poor writer had won numerous gold medals which he could not encash, but the old bugger was rich in a manner that the ordinary rich could never ever even dream of.

He had a young boy's love from a young mind.

The heart would be seen to soon if ever.

The above statement is because it is left to minds to allow their hearts to fall in love through words.

The writer, whenever he used to host small parties with his meagre funds in his derelict shack for rich beggars from gaudy areas encircling his slum begging for titbits of intellectuality, used to answer their laughing derisions at him being in hell with a question, "What are you enjoying in your heaven?" "Comfort!" used to be their uneasy answer, to which the writer used to laugh heartily and say, "In my hell, I have the enchanting discomfort of a creativity which hates comfort, for if there were comfort in my hell, my creativity would die a complacent death. I am alive in my hell while you are all dead in your heaven!"

The parties always used to end well even though the writer always rejected the scotch his guests used to bring and was happy with his poor drinks and rich thoughts.

The writer had understood a peace which was beyond the misunderstanding living. He knew that none were friends nor foes but only selfish beings. He had realized that to wait for acclaim from one was to invite negative declaim by the rest. And this ratio when inversed was just as true.

When life throws you a curve ball, curve yourself to avoid it. There is no need to hit it or anything else. Stupidity hits itself.

The young boy was beyond stupidity, for he was innocent, and stupidity does not manifest itself in innocence. It grows with knowledge and declines with wisdom.

The writer could not be called wise, as no one else can be, for he loved.

The writer's love was not the love of sex, but the love of the sex he could not have, the sex of procreation.

He loved the young boy as if he had come from his own loins.

But why had a simple answer. The young boy loved the writer's descendants, his books, and thus was one amongst them.

The writer had understood long ago that both men and women are selfish when it comes to their sexual desires manipulated by monetary desires.

Therefore, he had stood free with commercial sex workers whenever he could afford them, for, after all, all were the same, in one way or another.

This was his demise before old age got the better of him, him without a woman's love.

The ultimate question that the now old writer had never been able to answer was whether relationships were of the body or the mind, and if of both, which was superior.

However, the ultimate answer that he had not realized was that relationships do not exist at all and a human was to all tangible and intangible purposes all alone in all ways in the multiverse.

His ignorance of this ultimate answer made him love the physically unrelated but mentally connected young boy more than anything else in his world.

Love is ignorant.

The Escape

However, one fine night the old writer realized that his unexpressed love for the young boy was killing him. He decided to escape not caring about the young boy's search for him but knowing that the young boy would soon forget him once he did not find any new books of Anon and recover, for age was on the side of the young boy and not the old writer. The writer knew that if he stayed, he would be destroyed and destroy the young boy in the process too.

Mature love means letting go.

But innocent love has no idea of letting go.

When the writer left, he unknowingly exposed his identity to the young boy. Very soon, the boy cleverly put together the absence of the derelict at the derelict bookshop with the absence of Anon's books in it.

He cried so much in front of the bookseller one day while explaining why he was crying in-between deep sobs, that the owner of the bookshop came clean and told the young boy everything.

The young boy had grown a little physically since his affair with Anon had begun. He was now at a physical age where he was bold enough to run away, and Anon's books had made him smarter than most boys his age.

The young boy broke his piggy bank which was to all purposes a treasury and immediately ran to the railway station in his city with as much luggage as his chubby frame could carry, without a second thought as to what would befall his rich doting parents.

It is when we are young that we are the most adventurous as we are simply not afraid of what pitfalls may befall us.

It is then that we make the greatest progress in our short lives.

The boy had run to the railway station using the simple logic that the writer would not be able to afford any other kind of transport to escape him.

"Aren't you shorter than the ticket counter?" asked the smiling lady behind the desk.

"I am a midget," answered the boy in mock anger.

The delightful lady asked, "Where to, sir?"

The young boy had nerves of steel. He described the writer's physical characteristics and added that the old man had gone off his rocker and that their family had sent him to search for the old man. He asked the lady behind the counter to speed him on the way that his grandfather had taken.

There are many kinds of people in this world, out of which, there is but one adventurous kind which recognizes the adventurous, and sets them free if they are already not.

The lady behind the counter of journey was one of such, a free spirit.

She put the boy in a rich coach which was running on the same rails which had borne the burden of the writer and his thoughts.

A rich lady in the boy's coach was pleased with his pleasant appearance and started to ask too many questions while cooing indecipherably to decipher his background, "Whom do you love?"

A striking young man sitting beside the boy replied clearly to help him be free, "We are all in jails jailed by our loved ones. We have to break free of love."

Life lives in simplicity.

The more complex one makes it, the worse-off one is.

The boy asked, munching on a hard candy trying to make it soft, "Doesn't that mean we shouldn't be constrained in the first place, by love?"

The striking young man replied, "Love both constrains and liberates. You will not understand it now young one. Don't try to fly a kite without strings."

"Then won't my kite be totally free?"

"I would like to smack you!" laughed the young man who then took the young boy under his wing, realizing that he would from henceforth care for a sapling which would grow into a giant tree.

This young man in the coach of the young reader searching for the old writer had his own story like all else.

He was sick but unlike all men confronting death was not running away but was flying towards it.

In flight lies freedom, for you can circle your own death like eagles and understand it before you eat your way out of yourself with the help of vultures.

The young man got up and knocked on the rich lady's head while saying, "Knock, knock!"

The lady, completely taken aback by surprise, shouted, "Who is there?" and herself quickly answered, "Sex?"

This was an insane realization for the young boy, and he grew.

The young man asked the young boy, "Till where is your ticket to?"

"Till my stop."

"Where will you stop?"

"'When?' would be the better question."

"All right, when will you stop?"

"Once I have found my grandfather; myself."

The young boy had uttered this truth carelessly without realizing its import.

For, after all, we are but genes traveling in time.

And if a gene knows why it is what it is, that is after studying its history, it will be able to run forward better with its baton of the human.

The young man near death drew closer to the young boy, and said gently, "I will help you find yourself, your grandfather, don't worry."

The young boy was clever, "But don't ever try to steal my money, for I am the progeny of destiny."

Young people believe in a destiny which oscillates like a zillion pendulums crashing into one another and separating like lovers.

A station came and the train stopped, and since the young boy had no clue as to where his adopted grandfather had disembarked, he followed his future, the young man, and got off the train, which was exactly what the young man wanted.

We masochistically want our past to follow us.

The poor young man then asked the rich young boy, "Shall we eat? I am broke."

The young boy then realized his future was poor until he found his past.

The young boy paid for high tea and the two set off in search of the old writer where they were without knowing where he was.

We search for what we want inside of our spheres without realizing that the sphere has an outside where we should be actually searching, for what we are searching for always lies outside of our spheres.

The poor young man's past was a rich young boy whose past was a derelict old writer, a full circle.

But there was a hiccup in the circle. Neither was the young man a reader nor a writer. He was a disillusioned ordinary man who, though highly intelligent, was living life on life's terms, and not on his own ones. However, his intelligence had made him clutch at his past, the rich young reader, and made him want to search for the derelict old writer, so that the past, present, and future could be rich together.

He had stitched together a game plan from the moment he had met the young boy for a better future for all including the old writer.

The young man near death was an entrepreneur in life.

He wanted to celebrate the remainder of his life, and this should have been the motto of the rest of humankind.

Meanwhile, the writer was trying to get rid of the luggage that had been foisted upon him by himself. No matter how many distant stations from his hometown he got down at, he found the young boy gazing down at him from atop his shoulders.

Actually, the old writer had got down a few stops away from the stop at which the young ones had stopped.

Now, something made him traverse his path back.

This is the almost impossible probability which is a slightly possible improbability.

The three were destined to meet amidst the clanging of a zillion pendulums.

But it would not be soon or immediately a boon, if ever.

The writer had written a so-called children's story:

The Quiet Oasis

There was a pristine quiet oasis in the middle of nowhere in the desert.

It called out to nobody.

But the kafirs knew where it was and easily reached it while the religious were mesmerized by mirages of miraculous oases and could not make it to the real quiet oasis which along with its green palm tree friends and cool sands offered pure water, plenty of shade, and a soft bed to the weary during their journey.

Knowing is better than simply believing.

For, knowing is based upon solid reality while believing stands upon a shaky pedestal.

This was the story which had made the old writer highly infamous among the believing intellectual elite, but this was also the story which had made the young boy follow him.

The old writer often used to wonder about his quiet little oasis:

'Wasn't it within his desert?

'Wasn't it his peace where no beliefs led to?

'Wasn't it his and others' whose minds matched with his?

'Wasn't this quiet little oasis his piece of heaven on earth?'

The young boy was searching for his grandfatherly oasis while the old writer was waiting for his grandson's oasis to merge with his and be a respite for more and more kafirs.

To put it in simple terms, the grandfather and the grandchild wanted to live in peace together, far away from the corrupting society, and alone with their words written and read but never spoken.

This was a problem, but then again, "What is not a problem?"

But then again, "What is not a solution?"

'Problems are the children of the parents fear and desire.

'Problems arise simply because we want to be happy but cannot.

'Problems arise simply because we can't find happiness within ourselves.

'The quiet oasis within our deserts.

'And this is the solution.'

The old writer had asked himself, "Where can I find my peace?"

And had himself answered, "Within my absurdities and insanities!"

For life is both absurd and insane.

'What is love?' the writer when young had wondered.

'Pain and gain, for love's pain causes you to gain,' had been his own answer.

'But why?'

'Because, something so precious cannot be without its high price.'

The young writer had then cried himself to sleep.

Love is what you suffer.

Satan simply doesn't appear to everyone. He is in everyone. He was more so in the entrepreneurial young man who was hell-bent upon using the young boy's search for the old writer to find his own heaven.

The young boy was innocent, the old writer had transcended innocence, while the young man was experimenting with innocence.

This is but the way of the world.

Sticking to ideas makes one a fly trapped on flypaper. One is dead when one sticks on to one's ideas.

Life should be a river which flows around us washing us clean of our old ideas every moment, for life is anything but stagnant, and so our ideas should not be stagnant too.

One truth of life is that more never has enough and enough never has more.

It is tricky to traverse between the two, but it was exactly what the young man was doing. He was trying to walk between the more of the kid and enough of the grandfather.

The kid had never seen his grandparents and the grandfather who had made himself the kid's grandfather had never ever before seen a grandchild before the kid.

This love across generations would have remained a mystery if one had not understood the power of the word.

In the dark, of writers, books, and readers, these two had found themselves, and also, found themselves without each other.

The commercially minded young man would bridge the gap between the two, like a publisher.

Meanwhile, the old writer had realized that new empires are but built upon decimating, and not assimilating.

The writer was mad, as all good writers are, but what is madness?

True madness is but liberating oneself through song and dance, like a Krishna who is trying to forget his blues.

This is sanity in the form of accepted nudity.

Like Raja Ravi Varma's paintings.

It was Valentine's Day.

The old writer kept on receiving fraudulent calls on his cell phone.

Even though his cell phone kept on warning him that the calls he was receiving were fraudulent, he kept on receiving them in the hope that they were from his.

The old writer could not realize that hope was hopeless.

That was why he couldn't be a great writer.

But he was a good human being nonetheless.

He had written a story:

Toys

The child had many toys, with which to play his friends used to bring their own to his lavish home.

They used to pour all their toys into a huge bucket and after mixing them, used to pour all the bucket's contents onto a huge Persian rug so that all the toys were up for grabs.

Then the boys and girls used to rapidly hunt for the best commandos of war and the best dolls of sexual beauty in the mound of war and sexual beauty to make their own armies so that they could play them against their friends' with vivid imaginations blooming in their heads.

There were no telescopes and microscopes or Marie Curie dolls.

Stars and atoms were forgotten by the kids fed on war and sexual beauty.

What is the truth that all run after?

It is the truth of the lie of love.

The old writer knew that the small men and women of this world waste their time playing tiny games of one-upmanship. That is why he had decided to live great alone. But the young boy didn't know this, and was, therefore, bent upon destroying the old man's loneliness which the writer considered his solitude.

After a certain time, solitude turns into loneliness.

This is the way of the world.

The old writer was smart yet stupid while the young boy was simply innocent, which would absolve him of the crime of destroying the old man's so-called solitude when he found him, and the crime would actually turn out to be a great deed in destroying the old man's loneliness

But right now, they were poles apart, while their equator, the young man, was burning to bring them together in the hope that he would be a somebody in some way after melting and mixing the two poles.

The old writer's greatest wisdom came in the form of this children's story:

Happy Pond

There was a happy pond.

It was happy because all its denizens were happy.

Even the leeches, alligators, and snakes.

Meanwhile, the ducks, the frogs, the insects, and the birds, were on the brink of rebellion without the knowledge of the happy pond.

It was because each species was trying to sing its own song but was being distributed by the others'.

All had forgotten how to form an orchestra.

Thus, the happy pond became a sad pond, all because of intolerance.

All because of the lost harmony in the music of life.

The happy pond's denizens started eating each other and it became a cannibal holocaust.

The old writer had realized that man remains but a child and that truth can be fed to him only beakful by beakful from a mother's beak to a child's.

The writer had once wondered about love:

'Was it the body or the mind?'

And sex:

'Was it the body or the mind?'

He had then suddenly become enlightened and answered himself:

'Love in the mind need not be sex in the body and sex in the body need not be love in the mind.'

The writer had written:

Shady Tree

In a harsh desert, there was only one shady tree for miles and miles.

All animals of the desert wanted to rest in the shade of the shady tree once their hunting for food was over.

But they were too many, and since the shade was limited, they started hunting each other even when their hunt for their food was over.

The animals of the desert were hunting for shade even though none of them needed it, they being animals of the desert.

Each was hunting for a luxury it didn't need.

Soon, all the animals of the desert killed each other off in their hunt for a shade they didn't need.

Soon, the tree too died, for it served no purpose anymore.

Sharing should have been the solution.

But instead, infighting led to even the tree's shade's destruction.

The old writer had realized something that was always young and wicked like the mindless young:

We make simple mistakes and keeping them in mind for a lifetime, correlate them positively with the complex dirtier mistakes of others and feel more and more immensely guilty.

We are almost innocent. But when we unnecessarily extract and wrongly correlate, we become our own oppressors.

This truth which the writer had realized was only for his true readers who could be nothing but innocent.

The readers of certain writers form cults, and if the writer is good the cult will be best.

The old writer had lived long and had wondered, "Why sexual crimes?"

He had been a victim himself in a reverse way. The love of his life had committed a sexual crime against him by cheating on him.

But the question had arisen about sexual crimes.

And the writer had had but one answer, "Repressed is eternity suppressed."

He had also written in his adult books when young:

A repressed society which does not allow free love will be suppressed under sexual crimes.

Every man and woman wishes to be free with their love, emotional, or, and, physical.

No moral or judicial police have the right to restrain consensual sex, paid or unpaid, of any sort for majors.

The writer had been morally castrated for these thoughts of his.

But he was not defeated.

But he became old.

The writer had walked nowhere after this. For one needs to walk somewhere. One can't remain sitting. One needs a destination. But the writer walked nowhere, and miraculously, it was everywhere.

He had walked from the old into the arena of the young where child gladiators fought to die for the Caesar of creativity.

He had begun to write for the young, the young in whom the only future lay, even though he had none of his own young, and this was both his own solution and sacrifice for himself.

The old writer was bored with the God fallacy he had tried to eradicate.

Men were too scared of death to accept the truth about life.

Zero was the need of the hour for the number of Gods and not one, two, three, up to infinity for self-realization.

For all the men-created Gods did was divide and rule.

So, it was actually the men who divided and ruled; towards destruction.

Plain simple logic.

The old writer was tired, and giving up the shit that came with understanding, tried to be happy with his best friend Ignorance.

However, he had always known something:

That evolution was both fertilization and environment.

Genetics and epigenetics.

This was the core of his philosophy.

The old writer was a failed yet successful scientist. Shoonya. Nothing and Everything.

The old writer was an old fool who left his old man's scent of writing wherever he went.

Therefore, it was not long before the hounds of youth, the young boy aided by the young man found him.

And the mice had cornered a lion.

Philosophy Two

The old man when cornered in his hovel, roared, "I hid to escape your destruction at my hands youngling, but if you want to die for a noble cause, so be it. We two will set the world on a revolutionary path."

The young man whimpered, "What about me?"

The old man sighed, "You are above innocence and below wisdom. You will only be a soldier."

The young boy leapt into the old arms of the writer, and both physical weaklings fell on the harsh earth.

As the young man helped them both up, he said something to make him an inexcusable part of the trio, "We are always waiting for someone to appreciate us. But it is now time to make others fear us."

"For what?" whimpered the child, while the writer roared again, "For our ideas.

"If others have to fear us, we ourselves should not be afraid of anything. Be it mental or physical pain, pains which have as their root cause financial pain. And for financial pain to be eradicated in all of us requires equality. An equality that does not mean sameness. For that would be death, the death of creativity, the ultimate death.

"Nobody should be allowed to have more wealth than they need to be comfortable. Yachts and private jets are but a vile luxury."

"But how will the three of us achieve a Communist utopia?" cried the young man.

"In the only way we can, through writing for good readers," replied the old writer.

The child was scared lest his two comrades confiscated his rich purse.

It was twilight. The sky was all shades of subtle colours. There was an indefinable peace. There was an unbreakable peace. The old writer, who was lying prone on the ground, whispered into the leaning ear of his protégé, "It's a beautiful day to die. At least the last of the sun is shining upon me."

But the writer did not die, for how could he, for he had died innumerable times for innumerable stupid reasons.

For he loved.

But what did he love?

He loved to love and therefore he loved.

His lover had left him, but he had come across another writer whom he loved.

And when asked what that love was, he used to answer to none other but himself, that that love was for the pen of the mind.

None would understand him, for they lived in their loins and not in their minds.

But the writer was happy even though he was unhappy.

The writer had questioned himself innumerable times, "Why do we do all that we do?" and had finally come to the answer that it was all to escape the truth of birth and death.

And what was the truth according to him? His truth was that birth was accidental and death consequential.

He questioned himself again after his realization answering with another realization of his own:

"Do you have to be afraid to die?"

"You don't have to be. It comes, the all-enveloping narrowing tunnelling darkness, drawing you further and further in, until you scream, 'Save me God!'

"Either you will live or die.

"It is better to die, for you can be witness to infinity."

The foolish writer did not know that imagination for purposes other than creation leads to destruction.

But he persevered, in one direction or another.

The trio set upon a process of alchemy: trying to transform their thoughts into a pot of gold.

Not everyone can be born a prince. So, how can a true prince born in an ordinary family be a king? The writer had found an answer. If you can't have everything, be happy with nothing. Both are the same thing. There is ultimate freedom with both everything and nothing. Thus, the old writer was happy in his physical poverty and mental richness.

The writer had found the path to Nirvana during life itself. He lived like nothing mattered to him and nothing was his. This helped him to let go so very easily of mostly everything, and everything is but impermanent. Life included. But the writer was an addict. An addict to intoxicants. Thus, even while knowing and implementing the path towards enlightenment, he was not truly enlightened.

But in the boy, he found an innocence which he hoped would bring back his lost golden youth and steer him quickly and directly into the enlightenment he knew existed.

But there was another problem: his sex drive, the most common drive in the world of evolution. He strived against it day after day and lost each day.

Even with the youngsters witnessing his lack of control, he frequented commercial sex workers whenever he could, with the boy's money, but was never satisfied as his old love made him unable to satisfy himself.

The old writer was indeed a screwed-up person, and hence his innocent love for the innocent young boy.

And when in a dire need to vindicate himself, he helped the youngsters understand and pave the road to peace:

There are those who think, there are those who think and write, there are those who think, write, and talk, and finally, there are those who do all the before and act.

All the while he accepted his mistakes to the young hoping that they would not repeat them. But what is youth if not lost?

The writer, all his life, had failed in the last part, acting. It was not because he was a coward, but it was because he was brave beyond measure. He believed in non-action. He believed that life moves on a path of its own not deterred by any life. That no matter what you do or strive for, life will have its own way. This was not defeat, but acceptance. The writer's own life had taught him acceptance. To accept what he could never change.

So, what was the fun in life? The fun in life that the writer understood was to fight in spite of knowing you would be defeated. To carry your own cross like Christ. To enjoy being nailed to it. Masochism yes, loving each and every nail that was hammered into you with a love which transcended love for life.

"But why?" had the answer that you had to do it for other lives which did not have the power to suffer like you dear.

He told the young ones in a derelict shack which the three had made their home in:

You hear the koel in the warm and fragrant summer sun. It is neither singing for others nor for itself. It is singing simply because singing in the summer sun is in its nature.

And that was how and why the writer wrote. Simply because writing while being scalded was in his nature.

And nature undoubtedly is the most powerful being of all.

Whenever the writer used to get worked up about the wrongs done to him by one and all in the past, he used to tell himself and the younglings, "Whenever a negative emotion crops up, let go of it immediately, without trying to rationalize for or against anybody or anything, otherwise you will suffer and the perpetrator of the wrong on you will win."

Every time this happened, it was a long road to peace for him, but fortunately, with experience, the road to his peace was getting shorter and shorter, for the writer had walked a long and hard path throughout his life.

The old writer had long ago been totally fed up with ordinary people who had nothing more on their minds and in their bodies other than eating, copulating, and procreating.

His was a different sort of addiction: smoking, drinking, fucking, and above all, creating. The last but was the outcome of the first three.

Thus, he knew that he was not better than the rest, but only a delightful different. And this was enough to keep him moving towards wherever he was headed, for he himself did not know where he was headed.

This he made clear to his two comrades.

And one fine day, when things went from bad to worse inside the old writer's mind, with respect to the infidelity and betrayal he had had to suffer for almost half his life, he came to a beautiful conclusion which set him free. He concluded that men and women were free and could not be owned by anybody. They were free to flirt and fuck as they chose with anybody and everybody.

This devastating truth set the old writer free. Free from the bindings which turned ordinary men and women to rage and to pillage.

But what was the old writer's age? Now that we have been calling him old for so long, how old is he exactly?

They say that life begins at forty, and the old writer was just a little above that. But why old? Simply because his mind and body had both become old.

He had started to kill himself with his overthinking and drinking to overthink.

But now, though he wished to save the world with his immaculate thoughts, first and foremost, he wished to save himself by not thinking.

When young, relatively, the old writer had been irascible. When told to stop drinking, thinking, and writing, he had demolished all barricades to his fount of creativity, and had gone on intoxicating himself to find the fount of truth.

But by now, he had realized that there was no such thing as truth. That all was false. Neti Neti.

But one fine day he realized that there were possibilities, immense possibilities in the realms of being free and achieving great goals.

This was what the innocent and vibrant mind of the young boy had awakened in him.

The old writer's personal favourite was this story of his:

Nocturnal

The young male nightingale was a romantic. On most nights it deprived nature of its songs. But when the full moon rose, its muse, the young bird used to break out into an orchestra of its own.

The young bird knew that its frail wings could never reach Selene, but it was contented that full Selene shone upon it at least once a month, and the male nightingale was grateful for small mercies of nature, nature, which is the most loving of all creatures.

Meanwhile, Selene had no say in the matter. Her presence upon the poor young male nightingale who sang songs of life, philosophy, was constrained by nature, and nature can mean almost anybody and anything.

One full moon day, the sky was overcast with black clouds of jealousy. They hid Selene from the young nightingale.

He, the poor fool, died unable to sing, with his song caught in his throat and strangulating him until he was at a deathly peace.

The old writer had been beset throughout his life by those who craved the non-existent energy that drove itself through their birth and death.

He failed to explain to them the science of evolution, for they were all lawless fools, and science is but a set of laws.

The poor fools wanted immortality, and all that the poor writer had in his withered purse was mortality.

He used to tell the poor fools in the beachside bars beside the three comrades' derelict shack, "This is water with salt, sand, and bars beside.

"This is what you will get everywhere.

"Stop expecting something new unless you change yourselves."

Also, "Stop trying to impress strangers sitting at other tables, especially by talking out aloud your personal accomplishments.

"Nobody could care less, for all are screwed up in their own unhappiness trying to search happiness in the ocean.

"The ocean is within you and them alike, like salt water in blood.

"Be yourself. Let the ocean sweep you off your feet and drown you."

They all used to look at the writer as if he were a mad alien, except two who swallowed his every word like fish imbibing water in the ocean.

But the writer, who was always himself, did not care in the least, and always sat waiting for the girls who were promised him by the merchants of the beach.

But after the writer was done with the girls, he simply couldn't understand that what he was waiting for since his loss could prove to be such a loss, each and every time.

That wealth, woman, and land could be such disappointments.

He had struggled his entire life with technical virginity, and now that he kept on losing it, he couldn't even begin to imagine what he had had.

People are fools. Fighting for women. Nobody is worth it. It is just the same physical body.

Now that the writer was enlightened about the opposite sex, he had no more sex left in his body.

He had become enlightened.

People have so much and yet so less. They can talk about nothing but their hair, face, and body. Hairy!!!

That is why the writer wrote. To escape from the mundaneness of life.

His life was a rainbow in the shadow of life. He craved freedom. But the ultimate freedom lies only in death.

Once, standing on a lonely highway, in the midst of woods, the writer, after watching a few speeding cars, wondered, "Where are you headed human? In search of what happiness that lies inside you!"

He told his students once while enlightened with alcohol, which was always:

Fear is the driving force of the universe which can be replaced by strength if one is strong enough. Strength comes from freedom, and freedom comes when you begin to identify, understand, and then conquer the negative emotions which assail your mind and body and leave them quivering in the wind like a dying leaf. You may identify your negative emotions either through the mind or the body or both. They begin falling into a bottomless pit when hit by negative emotions, but one can instantaneously grow wings and fly back up towards the glowing sun if only one realizes how to let go instantaneously of negative emotions upon their advent.

The trick in life is to turn every defeat into a victory of oneself over oneself.

What they call as Karma is very simple to understand and also complex for obtuse minds.

If one is humble, and in a still energy state, then one knows that what happens with others who are in excited energy states trying, consciously or unconsciously, to hurt you, is of no consequence. Simply put, if you are in an energy state in which the whole universe wants to settle down in, the lowest energy state of peace, then even the whole universe can't hurt you with its unnecessary excited states. If you don't expect or hurt others, you are never hurt yourself.

Karma is within ourselves. It is nothing external. It is what we think and feel. Action and reaction all within us.

Another trick of life is to sit still and think. The whole universe will lay itself at your feet.

Nothing more to meditation other than not moving, either physically or mentally, except in the right direction after deliberation.

After all these thoughts, the foolish wonder whether we will become insensitive to the travails omnipresent in the world.

The answer is no, for negative emotions present adversities while positive emotions opportunities to overcome adversities.

Nothing has been achieved by negativity other than the Neti Neti of philosophy. Not this not that!

The very moment we embrace positivity, we become extremely sensitive while becoming stronger every moment, but if we let negativity to even touch us, we will have allowed insensitivity to sink deep within us. For, after all, it is only a weak person who is insecure and insensitive to the poorer part of the world.

Two men, or better yet, two boys conspiring to change the world into a communist utopia doesn't work, especially when they are almost always broke, and their third innocent comrade is comparatively rich beyond measure, and is being used by the other two, love or no love. This is also the case with the world. The problem also lies with the wiser elders being poor and the dumber youngsters being rich, which tilts the balance of power into wrong small hands. The poor older majority cannot win against the rich younger minority, for they have both age and money on their side. Grey cells don't stand a chance in the world against green bills and the reason has been lost in the annals of time.

How to change the world is a question that has haunted the best bodies and minds in time.

The best bodies tried to keep changing the world by eliminating lesser bodies, which was plain asinine, for it is more often than rare that the best minds are found in lesser bodies.

The best minds tried to keep changing the world by trying to change lesser older minds, fixed minds which they logically could not, and hence the best minds were logically the lesser minds, and the result was disaster for all as a result of wasted time, money, and energy.

But the writer was trying to change lesser younger minds which was the elixir for humankind.

The writer was the best human ever in spite of all his frailties.

The perfectionist writer had written a story about perfection:

Songbird

The young songbird had never given a public performance to date.

It had just tweeted incoherently with its head upon its parents' feathery chests till now.

But it had to sing for all of nature. That was its destiny from the moment it had hatched.

But today, in front of vastness, its tweets were more of threats to nature than a soothing song.

It was not because the tiny songbird, which had innumerable songs within it, did not know how to sing, but it was because the tiny songbird had had no experience and hence confidence in its own singing.

They would come with time, provided the tiny songbird kept on singing and thereby improving with every song until it became a big songbird whose voice would enthral the vastness which was awaiting its songs regularly.

But even today, the vastness applauded the tiny efforts of the tiny songbird and helped it to gain the confidence to keep singing and keep on improving.

Actually, the whole story was about self-actualization.

The old writer was damn good simply because it takes a whole load of skill to translate adult concepts into children's fables.

Ordinary life lies in extremities. People are always plus or minus one. But another trick of life lies in the average, Zero, Shoonya, Everything and Nothing.

For example, for ordinary people, sex is either primarily penetration or complete abstinence. They do not know the joy of exploring their partners' bodies and taking and giving joy at the same time.

The writer was laughed at, ridiculed, and deceived by the commoners because of his conviction in Shoonya, but he was a happy bugger who knew how to glean from the last grain of sand on an endless beach, joy.

The writer had never married because he had found the answers to why people marry:

Security:	Men and women want someone else to deal with their shit; both when young and old.
Sex and servitude:	Men want a sex slave and a servant to cook and clean up all kinds of their messes.
Death:	Parents hope to live on through their progeny and their progenies.

They want to relive their youth vicariously.

There was also a positive answer: Love!

But since the writer had been taught by life that there was no such thing as sexual love, he had been disappointed and never married.

The writer had once tried to earn money through other ways, but he had quickly realized that a soaring eagle could not be a flightless penguin, that there was a difference between the brilliance of the sky in the blazing sun and deep icy waters in which emotions went numb.

The writer had then decided that he would run the maze in the grooves caused by the towering grey cell mountains of his brain and exit his own thinking and philosophies completely someday to be totally free, free of both himself and the world.

As a result, the old writer lived by three simple rules:

1. Nobody can tell you what to do.

2. Nobody needs to appreciate what you do.

3. You don't have to explain yourself to anybody.

These three rules were a sure-shot way to poverty, and the old writer was indeed poor.

See and See
C and C

There was a staid little town of cows which was protected by tigers. Protected in the sense, ruled. It was beside the jungle.

The cows used to duly give milk, beef, and even veal to the tigers so that they may be allowed to lead a placid life.

But in the adventurous jungle beside the staid old town, there was the luxury of freedom. Even though those rebellious cows from the town, deer and other herbivores who came to slake their thirst at the watering hole were attacked and consumed by carnivores, the death toll was far lesser compared to the cows and calves who were daily on the menu for tigers who ran the show in the town.

The tigers were lazy yet crafty.

The cows dutiful and miserable.

The jungle was plentiful and adventurous.

In the jungle, more lived than died on account of all being free to live and die.

One fucking day, after the writer wrote this fucking shit, he told his boys:

> No more Communism and Capitalism for us you two deep shits. Enough, let us travel to come back to ourselves with more knowledge, and if possible, wisdom.

The two youngsters nodded until their heads almost fell off.

Travel

◇——◆——◇

All three then packed their meagre belongings and left the beach where their mind waves had made a home in.

When they were leaving, the writer was left cleaving:

The rich my young boy find poor quarters appealing as a result of rich quarters being boring due to their upbringing.

Young man, the poor find poor quarters depressing and rich quarters intimidating also as a result of their upbringing.

Let us try to find a middle path during our traveling.

The writer had understood the actuality that talking about mythology has no place in actuality.

The philosophy in mythology may be a reality, but only that reality which needs modification through evolution.

According to the writer, there was no point in digging up decayed skeletons and propping them up as your heroes clad in your robes.

This was a difficult concept to grasp by many and hence the writer himself was on the way to becoming a decayed skeleton during his life itself.

The Eaglet

The eaglet, from the very moment it hatched, hated the sun because of its blinding brilliance.

When it was kicked out of its nest, it flew downward and not upward, towards the sun.

But it could not find food simply because it flew too low.

It was starved.

It could not realize that the sun had to be harsh, and that it had to fly close to it, life, above the clouds, emotions, to be free, and well fed, for it is only from high above that we can realize the sustenance for our life from below.

We can only survive through the big picture.

The eaglet almost died, before it became an eagle, because of its non-conformance, but it finally managed to fly high and dive from high above and kill, before it died, to survive.

One has to fall, rise, and fall to live and succeed.

The writer wrote a song after a long while:

What you mean to me

Cannot be

But why should it be

For the universe itself cannot see

What we as the other see

> We will die in time
>
> It will be their crime
>
> That they could not allow us my friend
>
> To be a universal trend

And another

> I was walking downhill
>
> Amidst the forests of a hill
>
> Each tree wanted to tell
>
> Its own story and swell
>
> I told them that
>
> They were not from humans far apart
>
> Each of whom
>
> Wants to tell and bloom
>
> Like the writer I am
>
> Who is across rabid rivers a placid dam

There is a need, a dire need in all living creatures to express themselves. Some make beautiful things ugly and others ugly things beautiful.

This was clear to the trinity as they travelled in the subway. Teens with spray cans using rainbow colours and minds had turned the cars into both warzones and utopias. It was left to the beholder to differentiate between heaven and hell depending upon the state of his or her mind at the moment when he or she beheld the graffiti of underground Van Goghs.

Not everyone can be lucky enough to become a recognized artist, but everyone can be an artist. We have to learn from the graffiti artists that we can make our statements even in dark dungeons.

The writer in the subway talked to his young protégées:

How can a man be insensitive to the begging poor?

Simple, he blames it on the government.

And who chooses the government?

He who doesn't have a single penny for the poor.

A vicious recursive cycle.

True communism takes away both power and poverty, but unfortunately, both exist as a result of human tendency towards autocracy.

When the trinity disembarked the train, the old fool could not stop mouthing:

You are all flying kites using strings.

Try to fly your kites after cutting off their strings.

If you succeed, the kites are yours, else your kites are others' who find them in the trash.

"Are you at peace old man?" asked the young man with the young boy looking on in awe at all his elders' thoughts, words, and actions.

The old man stopped and set down his tiny backpack, "When you set down your entire baggage of thoughts, ideas, desires, expectations, relationships, and friendships, and walk ahead without looking behind at all that was never yours or even you, your true inner self, your only self, your true nature which is nothing but nature, will be one with streams, rivers, and waterfalls of water and flowers part of soft hills and towering mountains with their juvenile forests and gigantic jungles. You will be a bird, an animal, which exhilarates in being nature with the zephyr and the hurricane. You will be the tiny fish which swallows the ocean during a gale."

"What is the prerequisite for this beauty?" asked the exhilarated young boy.

The old man sighed, "Not what the young man and I have, but what you have, money and innocence. I am afraid that we both are snatching both from you."

The young boy couldn't decide whether to be happy or sad.

He fell into severe self-doubt, "Am I good or bad?"

His adopted grandfather told the young boy, "Nobody can judge you because they are not you. Be a touchstone, but of, by, and for yourself."

"Isn't that democracy?" asked the boy sucking on multiple lollipops he had bought for himself with his rich father's money.

The young man smacked the back of the young boy's head lightly, "You are a capitalist, idiot. Look at you gorging yourself on what is not food, spending a lot of money on junk food."

The young boy did not whine or cry, but continued his licking of various lollipops.

Taxi

The trio then quickly hired a taxi to just roam around using the boy's purse.

The young boy wanted to sit in the front beside the driver and so did the young man. Both got into a fight with childish screams fighting against a young man's ego which wanted to second-hand steer the trio to places he thought were best for the trio's enlightenment.

The old man intervened, "When you get into a fight, it is better to lose and walk away, for then the so-called victor's ego will destroy him, sooner than later, when he keeps on getting into fights, and eventually losing, for there is always a greater asshole, and the loser will eventually become the victor."

This led to all three riding uncomfortably in the taxi's backseat with the seat beside the driver empty.

There was no telling who won or who lost, either the empty seat or the argument.

During the drive to nowhere and everywhere, after the young man had made himself comfortable in the front seat beside the driver, with the young boy preferring the lap of his grandfather to sleep in, the old writer spoke in a whisper, "Philosophers are those who have lost in life and try to explain away their losses through arcane philosophies which carry no import for the common man."

The young boy lifted his head from the lap of his grandfather and asked, "Is there no truth then?"

"No", was the rude answer.

The young boy went back to sleep on his grandfather's lap with nightmares about life and death haunting him, while his grandfather couldn't sleep with his love haunting him through life and death which were both a part of existence.

The old writer had only one problem, but it was the biggest in existence, the Achilles Heel of great men. It was that, even though knowing, writing, and speaking the greatest of philosophies, he could not put even a single one of them into perfect action.

This fragility made him doubly human, and this enhanced human was way far superior to any hardened philosopher.

Now, one may wonder where the rich boy's father was during these episodes starting from the young boy fleeing his home in search of the old writer, his adopted grandfather.

The rich man had been at his son's heels most of the times, but when the Three Musketeers vanished into poor places, living frugally off the rich young boy's rich purse, the rich father's rich purse lost track of them. It was simply because the father did not understand poverty or how people lived in it.

Therefore, even though the father came very close to his son most of the times, he was unable to catch hold of him.

In poverty, men lose their identities, and become one cloaked by the cloak of poverty. There are no individuals.

Rich people have separate identities based upon their works, wealth, and positions, but poor people are identified only as the poor as their works are considered to be so small so as not to give them individual identities. Neither do they have wealth nor positions.

Thus, there is a blanket ban on the individual identities of the poor.

That is why the father could not find his son.

But the old writer was very well aware that they were being hunted, and that only he and the young man would suffer on being caught with the young boy.

So, he warned the young man in the front seat, "Be careful of the places we choose to visit. None of them should agree with the boy's desires, for his father will be knowing his son's desires."

"But we are using his money," squirmed the young man on his seat, even though he had wanted to dictate the places the trio would visit.

"The boy will grow all the more wiser by not getting what he wants," quietly laughed the old writer, and began writing another story:

The Solitary Eagle

The eagle soared alone.

Neither did it require another to survey the vastness that it did with nor to hunt with.

The clouds were its to fly into and escape above, all the while shuttling between blindness and omniscience.

No friend could match it in its omnipresence or omnipotence over its hunting grounds.

A second was not needed.

For once a second comes, the superior will have to slow down for the inferior.

The eagle was its own God and it would brook no worshippers.

For what kind of a God is a God who wants followers and is not free of every kind of adulation and expectation?

The taxi was purring along snaky roads with gigantic trees soldiering the way towards freedom.

The old man sighed as the child got up from his lap rubbing its big eyes, "To be free, understand every thought when it arises, as to from where it arose, why it arose, how it arose, and kill it immediately."

"Isn't that a bit insensitive?" yawned the young boy.

"I will educate you about sensitivity," softly said the old writer.

"We will never know how much we hurt others at any moment of time, so we should be understanding when others hurt us.

"Hurt should be forgiven by mature minds because it is caused by puerile minds."

The taxi driver applauded with both hands letting go of the steering wheel and almost caused an accident.

The taxi driver was a garrulous fellow. He beamed, "You seem to be a writer old man, right?"

"Yes," sighed the writer.

"What is a writer?" asked the driver, escaping from his garrulousness.

"Not what but who. A writer is one who orders the thoughts which are common to everyone yet not understood by everyone in a written manner so impeccable so as to provide enlightenment to the ones who read him."

The driver once more almost caused an accident.

He then said he was hungry.

The writer then spouted about hunger:

Hunger arises in one who is really starved; really starved for the truth or food or both.

Real starvation is for food, and pseudo starvation is for truth.

One can find the solution to starvation of either the body or the mind by choosing which one to satisfy.

If one wants to satisfy both, one will die of starvation.

The young man asked, "Which form of government is better suited to stave off starvation? Capitalism or Communism?"

The writer replied with a laugh, "The basic duty of a human lies neither in Capitalism nor Communism, but in the duty to be a happy human, either good or bad. A happy human will never starve, for his mind, not dwelling on unnecessary things, will be more than active to feed his body."

The writer then digressed and burst into a poem:

Mortal mortal you are mortal

Yet you scream immortal

But don't you realize dutiful

That just as you are sinful

You are also beautiful

More as a mortal

The writer then became sad, "As the past draws to a close, and the deathly future closer to the uneasy present, one realizes the futility of love, sex, and everything else."

Hunger vanished from everybody's minds, but not their stomachs.

The writer and his younglings halted at night in a hotel and were given rooms on the second floor. There was no elevator in the dingy hotel.

The night they halted, the writer made a fool of himself with the driver by drinking too much and getting into a bar fight.

In his drunken enthusiasm, he lifted a heavy barstool to smash the enemy into smithereens and became his own worst enemy.

He sprained his back, the barstool fell from his hands, and he on the floor.

He could not get up from the floor. The pain was excruciating, making him shake from limb to limb.

But then there was a miracle. The clear-eyed and clear-faced young boy, who had been watching his adopted grandfather's juvenile shenanigans, bent down beside him, and clasping his frail old hand firmly in his strong young one, made him get up, and took him up the stairs to his room.

Here strength was a matter of innocence and spirit, which the young boy possessed in abundance compared to the old writer's rapidly dwindling ones.

That night, the writer realized what true love actually was. It had nothing to do with the opposite sex, but to do with innocence.

Later, lying on his bed, the old fool mixed an overdose of painkillers in lots of cheap whiskey and swallowed the whole in one gulp, and as he was falling asleep, his mind started wandering more and more:

> He realized that the imaginary God was a real threat to world peace.
>
> That life is one endless quest for a perfect mate.
>
> That living with the truth of death, nothingness, is true living.

The writer got up in the middle of the night, thinking about his love. Both his body and mind were in agonizing pain. He started crying and diluting his cheap strong whiskey with his pristine tears, prolonged his agony. He was a masochist to his core.

There is only so much that even the strongest can endure, and the writer blanked out before dawn. The empty glass fell down from his hand and shattered on the uncarpeted floor.

Found

When he woke up with an agonizing hangover, he was still not free from his philosophy.

Lying on his bed, he shouted, "To be insensitive to others is to be sensitive to oneself.

"For all lowly scum are following the same philosophy, even though they are not philosophers, but only lowly scum."

The old writer got up on his shaky legs governed by an unsteady mind.

The broken pieces of glass beside his bed punctured the soles of his feet and let out rich red blood. But his deadened mind was impervious to physical pain.

He searched through the empty bottles strewn around his room to find at least a sip in a carelessly emptied one.

To his luck or bad luck, he found three with enough sips left in them to make his mind and body steady.

To himself, he said, 'Enough! Why should I care for the boys? The pain I do not feel is my best companion.'

He then, forgetting to wear his slippers, walked out of the hotel leaving behind him footprints of blood.

His younglings, after they woke up, and not finding their mentor in his room, followed his footprints of blood, and soon found him sleeping blissfully in a gutter.

What causes a man to come to such a state? Simple, the conflict between lost love and found love which one is afraid will be lost leaving one hollow both inside and outside.

The young boy ran and bought mineral water to splash upon and refresh the writer lying in gutter water.

When the writer came to his senses, he answered an unasked question, "This is the dirty pain which brings pristine beauty to my writings."

The young boy started crying while saying, "Then I don't want you to write anymore. You come and live in my home. I don't want to read any more books by Anon. After seeing and living with Anon, I realize that he doesn't practice what he preaches. His philosophy is not practicable even by himself."

The old writer started crying, this time not diluting whiskey by his tears, but gutter water, making it pure.

The young man sighed, and rising, said goodbye. The young boy stopped him and said, "Even though you are going to die young, you are still young. Live it. You can work in my home."

Now, since this is a novella, a story, a story which had better be happy, the young boy's father, who had followed the trinity to the hotel by morning, and who all along had been standing behind the trinity in the gutter without their knowledge, happily said, "So be it!"

All four soon found themselves in the young boy's mansion with his mother in happy tears.

Philosophy Three, The Final Goodbye

The taxi driver left after leaving them. He had none to call his except the road. The money he earned was nothing except what kept him alive on the road.

We all move on leaving others behind. We have nobody and nothing except ourselves and our lonely journey. We earn to eat, mate, and survive so that we can keep on moving to do the same.

We are all drivers of taxis. Our destinations are the destinations of passengers who do not care for us. The ones we serve are the ones who betray us for pennies. We do not have our own destinations because we love our passengers and also because we need to earn and stay alive. Earning need not be money but the honey of love, and that is where the drivers of life taxis fail. They do not drive an empty car to their own destinations. They feel the need to fill their vehicle of life with loved ones. Such an overloaded car is destined for an accident in which the only fatality is the driver, the writer.

Once the three had scraped off their dirt of poverty and were relaxing in luxury with the owner of the mansion beside which the derelict writer's shack stood in a slum, the writer, after taking a sip of his rich host's scotch, instead of gulping it like the cheap whiskey he used to drink, sighed with pleasure, and said sitting on luxurious upholstery, "Give me luxury and I will give you wisdom."

He then bent forward and polished off his scotch leaning back.

The young boy's father immediately leapt to attention and refilled the glass of the drunkard who thought he was a genius.

It is absolutely ridiculous what doting fathers do for their sons.

The writer did not touch his scotch, but brought forth his newborn philosophy, "I was an atheist. I am one still.

"But think. Think deeply. Can science explain what an atom is? Can it explain why an electron, positron, and neutron? Why they have to be what they are?"

The writer then got up and left with his full glass of scotch untouched, leaving all in the large plush room intoxicated.

The next morning, at the rosewood breakfast table, when the hungry writer was reaching greedily for a dish with both hands, his sleeves slipped back.

The rich father had not become rich so easily. He was in the habit of observing practical things, unlike the writer who was always absorbed in the abstract.

The father calmly asked, "What are these slash and burn marks on your wrists and forearms?"

The hungry writer stood up straight and asked softly, "Is it a crime to love and suffer?"

The rich man, who had never known true love, said tearfully, "I am proud of my son. He is better than me, for he found and has you for a Guru."

All had a hearty breakfast, the writer's raised sleeves notwithstanding.

The elders then sat chewing fat cigars and talked about powers.

The writer laughingly told his host, "You are the king and I am the prince.

"The best power is no power.

"A power without responsibilities.

"I can screw a commercial sex worker with freedom while you with all your money are inhibited because of your power.

"I, the powerless, am more powerful than you!"

The rich man retorted, "Is your life only about drinking and fucking?"

The writer laughed out loud and responded, "Pray tell me what else you and your brethren are doing?"

"We work for the common good."

"Of whom?"

The rich man got agitated, "For the derelicts like you, of course!"

The writer laughed harder, "And what do we do?

"You yourself said it!"

The young boy who was always a part of his father started crying, not understanding, but sensing, the import of the matter being discussed.

The elders felt ashamed and dispersed to their quarters, with the dying young man having kept his silence, for he knew that when one has to eventually die, there is no point in winning any argument.

None attended lunch much to the distress of the mother.

But all were hungry by dusk and thirsty too. The three elder males chose an old wine and sat with it.

Like the superb red wine, the discussion was pleasantly dry, initially, but it soon got wet.

The young man finally decided to be young once more, and tried to flirt with the pretty maid who was coming to serve them appetizers before dinner.

"Isn't she beautiful?" asked the unlucky rich man whose wife was busy making up her hair in their bedroom.

The young man became abashed, while the old writer on intellectual wine became smashed, "Everybody is beautiful, ugly or beautiful, and beauty depends only and simply upon whether you yourself are ugly or beautiful."

The young boy rushed into his adopted grandfather's outstretched arms and hugged him.

What do we know of a child's mind even though we were once young too!

The father, who had never seen his son so happy, smilingly asked his adopted father, "So, you have finally found your calling..."

The philosopher answered, beaming, "There is no calling, only doing, dealing with what is forever coming."

The mother entered, "You are talking about family Mr Writer. Do you have one other than my son and husband?"

"Had or have, in whichever way you choose to look at me and my life.

"My life is an open book free for dissection and discussion by each and every vulture.

"Shall we eat?"

After a scrumptious dinner, the three elder males sat over brandy and cigars accompanied by other hells as well.

The old writer, as was his habit, began philosophizing unnecessarily, "The problem with man and mankind is that they try to find meaning in meaningless things, very often the constructs of meaningless people trying to find meaning in meaningless things."

"Answer in one word your explanation of your philosophy," goaded the younger the older.

"God," replied the older to the younger and left the room to sleep the sleep of babies, but he did not have the privilege of lullabies.

The next dawn, when the writer decided to become a walker, to improve his health, and went for an early walk, the father, who had not slept the entire night, leapt at the chance to catch the philosopher at his fresh best, and doggedly pursuing him, asked, "You are greatly gifted, aren't you?"

The writer, without taking even a single pause between his strides, replied strongly, "There is no gift in this universe. You have to earn every tiny bit of fame or infamy."

The father, upon hearing this, halted in his tracks, while the writer went on with his walk outside his once slum on polished roads.

Do we ever truly return to our homes?

The writer, on that bright dawn, during his happy walk, wrote a dark story in his mind with a happy ending:

The Blind Cell

A baby was born in a cell with a locked door and no natural light.

Its mother died during childbirth.

It was born in servitude to artificial light and jailers.

How are we any different?

We are born in the prisons of our families with their artificial beliefs.

Our truth dies with our birth.

We are all servants to constructs and their constructors.

How can we escape this blind cell we are in?

Simple, through Zen.

Open your eyes and that's it.

You are in vast fields of golden-green, running through dense vegetation of wheat easily giving way for you to go through, with the sun on your face and the wind in your hair.

Open your eyes and you are free in paradise.

The prisoner in his blind cell was suddenly transported into freedom.

The writer, as his feverish feet walked faster and faster, let his mind do the same:

Is your heart so small that it has room in it for only one person?

Your heart was small.

That only person who was small too easily shattered it.

But great edifices are built out of the ruins of decrepit hovels.

Remember, you are the architect of your dreams and their actualization; your self-actualization.

Soft hearts, which are a sign of noble upbringing, are easily broken, but strong minds, which are the result of great teachings, go on to build supreme empires of the mind.

In such empires, neither friends nor foes have a say, unless their minds are equal to yours.

A lover is both a strength and a weakness.

It depends on you who loves how to love, but most importantly, whom and what to love.

When to love is never a question at all, for you always have to be in love with someone, something, or the other to accomplish anything great.

Be a lover, but remember, love is not sex and sex is not love.

Desires, even the smallest desire is detrimental to one's peace, even the desire for peace, but without desire, no being can exist.

So, like all else in life, there are good desires and bad desires.

It is impossible to classify desires absolutely as either good or bad, for each individual, as has already been said, is an individual. For the thick of the head, everyone is unique with his or her own unique good and bad desires.

No man is a criminal except according to the laws of the society he is born in.

A man may be lucky to be born in the freedom of Amsterdam or unlucky to be born amidst the many a ban of the Taliban.

No man has a choice in his birth, but he should have every choice as to where he wants to live and what he wants to do.

Now, if the question arises about rapists, torturers, and murderers, it is obvious to any sane individual that these anti-social elements cannot survive in any society.

However, it is a harsh truth that non-sapiens, unwise people who belong to the genus Homo, are wreaking havoc in the name of Gods and religions. They are the worst homicidal maniacs who do not understand the difference between the words believing and knowing.

Now, coming back to desires after digressing quite a whole lot, the only good desire is a desire to do good, always, and the only bad desire is a desire to feel good, always. True altruism is true masochism.

Suddenly a bird in the trees sang and something fell upon the walker writer's head.

He stopped in mid-tread, and disgustingly ran his hand over his long hair screwed-up about the shit he was sure he would encounter.

But instead, a beautiful pristinely white flower, gifted by the tree in whose foliage the happy bird was singing joyously, fell off his hand supposedly cleaning his still lustrous long hair onto the rich brown earth.

The writer was shocked out of his stupid philosophy and immediately came to practicality.

He slowly bent down and gently picked up the beautiful flower which had died so that he could understand the beauty of life, and said to no one in particular but to everyone in general, "Life is beautiful!"

The writer rushed back to his grandson's home, and shaking awake the young boy who had had enough of his grandfather's eccentricities, shouted into his sleepy ear, "Don't wait for somebody to write your story when you are dead.

"Instead, write your own epic while you are still alive and kicking."

He then ran out of his adopted grandson's home with his backpack which he had still not unpacked.

He vanished from the young boy's home, leaving in his care the dying young man, into nothingness like all of us will some day, but having become enlightened.

FINIS